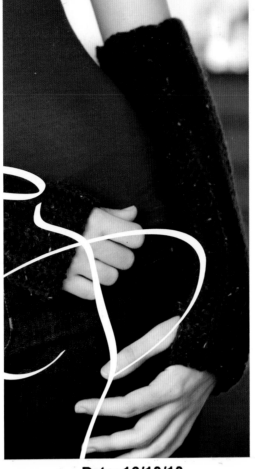

Date: 12/10/13

746.434 HAL
Hall, Mary Jane.
Crochet that fits : shaped
fashions without increases ...

CROCHET *that fits*

SHAPED FASHIONS WITHOUT INCREASES OR DECREASES

MARY JANE HALL

kp

Cincinnati, Ohio

WWW.MYCRAFTIVITY.COM
CONNECT. CREATE. EXPLORE.

**PALM BEACH COUNTY
LIBRARY SYSTEM**
3650 Summit Boulevard
West Palm Beach, FL 33406-4198

W9-AMO-151

metric conversion chart

TO CONVERT	to	MULTIPLY BY
inches	centimeters	2.54
centimeters	inches	0.4
feet	centimeters	30.5
centimeters	feet	0.03
yards	meters	0.9
meters	yards	1.1

fw

F+W PUBLICATIONS, INC.

Crochet That Fits: Shaped Fashions Without Increases or Decreases. Copyright © 2008 by Mary Jane Hall. Manufactured in China. All rights reserved. The patterns in this book are for the personal use of the reader. By permission of the author and publisher, they may be either hand-traced or photocopied to make single copies, but under no circumstances may they be resold or republished. It is permissible for the purchaser to create the designs contained herein and sell them at fairs, bazaars and craft shows. No other part of this book may be reproduced in any form or by any electronic or mechanical means including information storage and retrieval systems without permission in writing from the publisher, except by a reviewer who may quote brief passages in a review. Published by Krause Publications, an imprint of F+W Publications, Inc., 4700 East Galbraith Road, Cincinnati, Ohio, 45236. (800) 289-0963. First Edition.

Other fine Krause Publications books are available from your local bookstore, craft supply store or online retailer, or visit our Web site at www.fwpublications.com.

12 11 10 09 08   5 4 3 2 1

DISTRIBUTED IN CANADA BY FRASER DIRECT
100 Armstrong Avenue
Georgetown, ON, Canada L7G 5S4
Tel: (905) 877-4411

DISTRIBUTED IN THE U.K. AND EUROPE BY DAVID & CHARLES
Brunel House, Newton Abbot, Devon, TQ12 4PU, England
Tel: (+44) 1626 323200, Fax: (+44) 1626 323319
Email: postmaster@davidandcharles.co.uk

DISTRIBUTED IN AUSTRALIA BY CAPRICORN LINK
P.O. Box 704, S. Windsor NSW, 2756 Australia
Tel: (02) 4577-3555

Library of Congress Cataloging-in-Publication Data
Hall, Mary Jane.
Crochet that fits : shaped fashions without increases or decreases / Mary Jane Hall. -- 1st ed.
p. cm.
Includes index.
ISBN-13: 978-0-89689-662-8 (pbk. : alk. paper)
ISBN-10: 0-89689-662-5 (pbk. : alk. paper)
1. Crocheting. 2. Clothing and dress measurements. I. Title.
TT825.H25628 2008
746.43'4--dc22

2008029164

Editors: Stefanie Laufersweiler, Toni Toomey
Cover design/Art direction: Clare Finney
Interior design: Melanie Warner
Production coordinator: Matthew Wagner

Photographer: Ric Deliantoni
Wardrobe stylists: Robin Fields, Mary Murphy
Illustrator: woolypear

ABOUT *the* AUTHOR

mary Jane Hall has been crocheting for thirty-eight years and has taught more than sixty people how to crochet. She specializes in crochet fashion design and is a Professional member of the Crochet Guild of America (CGOA). Mary Jane is passionate about crochet and loves designing trendy wearables. She designs full time and has had many of her original designs published in various books and magazines. She has given the talks "How to Get Published" and "Designing Tips" to local crochet groups, including the Dayton, Ohio, chapter of the Crochet Guild of America.

Originally from Texas, Mary Jane currently lives in Ohio. She has been married for thirty-eight years, and she and her husband, Terry, have three grown children who are all married and have families of their own. They enjoy their grandchildren, who are a huge part of their lives. Mary Jane manages a "free" clothing store, called United Voluntary Services, which clothes more than 1,500 people in their county every year.

Mary Jane's first crochet book, *Positively Crochet: 50 Fashionable Projects and Inspirational Tips*, is currently available. Visit Mary Jane's Web site at www.mjcrochet.com.

This book is dedicated to all the new and experienced crocheters out there who have been a little scared of making their first crocheted garment. I know you do not want to be stuck making scarves, pot holders or afghans for the rest of your life. You, too, can enjoy making crochet wearables, and it is my desire that you experience the same joys I do by making something for yourself or others you can be proud to wear. I believe this book will open up a whole new world to the beginning crocheter or to the person who has thought they could never make crocheted garments. It's much easier than you may think!

acknowledgments

This book would not have been possible without book acquisitions editor Candy Wiza, who believed in me and encouraged me the past year while I was writing my first two books. Any time I was stressed or discouraged, she was ready to encourage me and lift me up.

I would like to thank my family and friends for being so patient and loving with me while I worked on this book. I started it immediately after my last book was sent to print, and it has taken many long months to finalize everything. It has not been easy, and I appreciate the fact that they all believe in me and have been there to cheer me on!

Much of my determination and steadfastness came from my precious mama: I followed in her footsteps of realizing a dream by authoring books. And, Daddy, I know you are looking down from Heaven, proud of me. I'd like to thank my sisters, Judy and Donna, who helped me review this book and gave valuable input when I needed a second opinion. I will not forget all the encouragement you gave me. Thank you, Terry, my dedicated husband and friend, for being patient with me and for all the times you did grocery shopping and household chores while I was busy at the computer or designing a project for this book.

I also want to thank my three wonderful children and their spouses, who are all precious to me. Brian and Anca, thank you for understanding when I had to focus on this book. Jamie and Virgil, thanks for encouraging me; Tracy and Ashley, thanks so much for believing in me. Of course, I must mention the sweetest, cutest grandchildren on this earth: Jade, Chloe, Sophia and little Coen. I love you all so much!

I want to thank all the pattern testers who were willing and eager to help me out, and the contract crocheters who restitched items in a different color to be photographed for the book. Thanks so much to: Rachel Berent, Karen Blumberg, Yvonne Bowser, Adrienne Clark, Alyssa Denen, Pam Frye, Christy McMahon, Judy Morrison, Aminta Moses, Maclana Mowry, Sharon Mowry, Kimberly Stevens and Annette Stewart. And a special thanks to my friend Cindy Gillespie, who was there to make sure everything went smoothly when putting the final manuscript together. I truly could not have done this without all of you!

Last but not least, I want to thank my editors, Susan Lowman, Toni Toomey and Stefanie Laufersweiler, and the entire staff at Krause Publications for their hard work related to the publication of this book.

TABLE *of* CONTENTS

INTRODUCTION

crochet's beginnings: bright and boxy

Is your concept of crocheted garments the stiff and boxy creations of the past? Flip through books from the 1940s and '50s and you'll find crocheted garments tastefully done with smaller yarn or thread. Crochet experienced a huge boom in the '60s and '70s, and with it came the bright (sometimes garish) color combinations of the day that some crocheters say gave the craft a bad name.

This was also the time that inexpensive acrylic yarns were introduced, which helped make crochet affordable to the masses. But, when crocheted with a hook that is too small, these yarns have all the comfort of a straitjacket. Still, when I flip through my crochet magazines and almost every crochet book I have from that era, I see some fabulous designs that remain popular and fashionable today.

crochet for today: a formed fit that flatters

I am one of a growing number of designers who has set a goal of trying to reverse the myth that crochet cannot possibly be comfortable *and* flatter the figure. If you picked up this book because the sophisticated number on the cover caught your eye, I hope I can convince you further with the projects inside. If you are a knitter who has turned away from crochet in the past because of its reputation for being stiff and unflattering, I hope I can change your mind. I personally love the look, feel and fit of knitting, but I'm addicted to the fun of crocheting and all the amazing lacy designs that can be created with no other craft.

In this book, I will show you how to crochet garments (and accessories) that are not only soft and drapeable but fitted and flattering by using my unique Graduated Stitch Method—combining stitches of varying heights within the same row—with the right size hook and yarn. Even beginners can make fabulous shaped yet simple crocheted clothing with this method, which eliminates the need for the sometimes complicated process of using increases and decreases (the addition or subtraction of stitches) to give a piece its shape.

old stitches, new method

Nearly all the stitches used in the book's projects are not new, but my method is very nontraditional in the way the items are formed. Most of the wearables in this book are not unusual or unique in the way they are styled. What *does* make them different is the way the designs are created and how they get their shape. Instead of the cumbersome and sometimes confusing task of crocheting in the round, you use graduated stitches to construct each item. With my method you are essentially creating garments with squares and rectangles, but the finished item does not appear that way.

Graduated stitching is also what helps mold a piece to the body if you desire a fitted look. Placing shorter stitches on the same row as taller stitches causes the piece to "cup" in at certain areas, resulting in a form fit without the hassle of figuring out increases and decreases. In fact, you won't find a single increase or decrease in this book.

If you prefer a looser fit than what is shown in the project photos, I offer simple instructions for adjusting each garment to your taste.

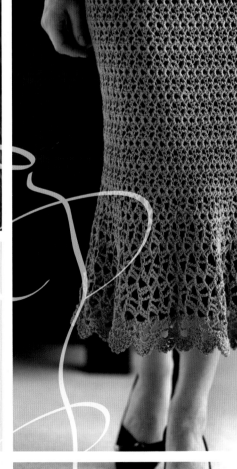

custom-fit creations to your size and shape

This book provides patterns and instructions for making garments for sizes up to an adult 3X. Most of the items in this book can easily be made to fit a toddler or child as well by following the additional instructions given.

Even though I list actual stitches and the number of rows needed to make these garments up to an adult size 3X, I also show how to create any project from scratch without having to follow a pattern and how to custom fit it to your unique body. After all, every individual's body shape is different. A longtime complaint of many plus-sized crocheters is that the patterns they have used just do not fit their shape, no matter what size they make. A woman with a classic pear shape may end up with a garment that's too small in the hips or too large in the bust area. I believe the method of graduated stitching I've created will change all of that and help eliminate those frustrations.

same start, different endings

A big benefit of the projects is that several different pieces can be made from the same fundamental design. The basic capelet in the first chapter can become a skirt, hat or even a purse. Some projects call for a different-size yarn and hook, but you'll still be able to build all those items from the same basic pattern. I tell you how to adjust many of the designs in the book to create entirely new items. The baby-doll top on page 96, for instance, can be modified to make a lacy skirt of any length or a little girl's dress, using the same technique and shape.

I draw upon my sewing background to offer finishing touches such as weaving tiny elastic through the edge of a top to help it stay on the shoulders, as opposed to decreasing in that area as you normally would for the same effect.

bye-bye, blankets!

Maybe you've thought you are destined to make only scarves, pot holders or afghans for the rest of your crocheting days. This book is dedicated to showing beginners and advanced crocheters alike that you *can* make projects that go beyond a simple square or rectangle.

You may have felt intimidated by patterns for shaped garments that require increases, decreases or working in the round. I hope those days are gone forever as you try my new method of graduated stitching and learn how to make flattering fashions the easy way.

abbreviations guide

abbreviation	meaning
approx	approximately
beg	beginning
blo	back loop only
ch(s)	chain(s)
cont(ing)	continue(ing)
dc	double crochet
dtr	double treble (yarn over 3 times)
flo	front loop only
hdc	half-double crochet
hdtr	half-double treble
htr	half-triple crochet
lp(s)	loop(s)
opp	opposite
oz	ounce(s)
patt	pattern
pm	place marker
rem	remaining
rep(ing)	repeat(ing)
rnd(s)	round(s)
RS	right side(s)
sc	single crochet
sk	skip
sl st(s)	slip stitch(es)
sp(s)	space(s)
st(s)	stitch(es)
tog	together
tr	triple crochet (yarn over 2 times)
V-st	V-stitch
whip st	whip stitch
WS	wrong side
wt	weight
yo	yarn over (wrap yarn around hook)

Throughout the book you will see abbreviations for crochet terms and other words that appear frequently in the instructions. After you've been crocheting a while, you will remember the terms without needing to refer to this list, but it's helpful when you're first beginning.

stitches to know

Many of the stitches used in these projects are common in crochet, but also shown are some lesser-known taller stitches that are tremendously helpful when making shaped garments with the Graduated Stitch Method. You may be familiar with triple crochet and the double treble, but even very experienced crocheters may have never heard of a half triple or a half-double treble.

chain (ch)

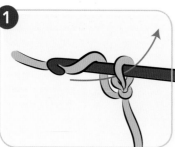
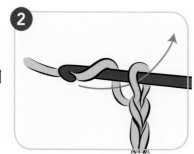

After placing the hook through the slip knot, wrap the yarn around the hook. Draw the yarn through the lp on the hook (1 ch made). Repeat this step.

slip stitch (sl st)

Insert hook into the st or sp indicated, yo to create a lp on the hook. Draw lp on hook through both the st indicated and the lp on the hook so that only one lp remains on the hook.

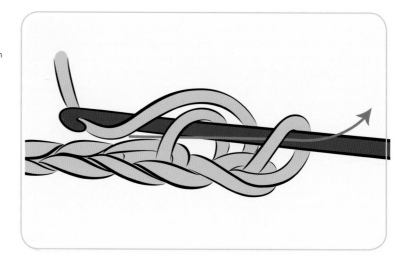

single crochet (sc)

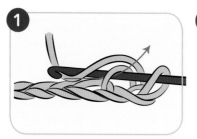

Insert the hook into the st or sp indicated, yo and pull the new lp through

the st only. Yo again and pull a lp through both lps on the hook. One lp

remains on the hook (1 sc made).

half-double crochet (hdc)

Yo once, insert hook in st or sp indicated, yo and draw up a lp, yo and draw through all 3 lps on the hook.

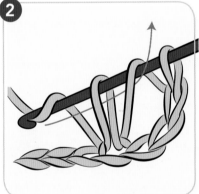

double crochet (dc)

Yo once, insert hook in st or sp indicated, draw a lp through this st to make 3 lps on the hook, yo again and draw a new lp through the first 2 lps on the hook (2 lps rem on the hook), yo again and draw a new lp through both lps on the hook (1 dc made).

stitches to know

half-triple crochet (htr)

Yo twice, insert hook in designated st, yo and draw up a lp (4 lps on hook), yo and draw through 2 lps on hook (3 lps on hook), yo and draw yarn through all 3 lps on hook.

triple crochet (tr)

Yo twice, insert hook in designated st, yo and draw up a lp (4 lps on hook), yo and draw through 2 lps on hook (3 lps on hook), yo and draw through 2 lps on hook (2 lps on hook), yo and draw through both lps on hook.

half-double treble (hdtr)

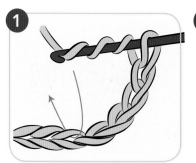

Yo 3 times, insert hook in designated st, yo and draw up a lp (5 lps on hook), yo and draw through 2 lps on hook (4 lps on hook), yo and draw through 2 lps on hook (3 lps on hook), yo and draw through all 3 lps on hook.

double treble (dtr)

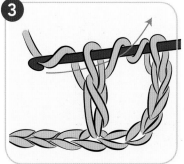

Yo 3 times, insert hook in designated st, yo and draw up a lp (5 lps on hook), yo and draw through 2 lps on hook (4 lps on hook), yo and draw through 2 lps on hook (3 lps on hook), yo and draw through 2 lps on hook (2 lps on hook), yo and draw through both lps on hook.

checking your gauge

Gauge is the measurement of your stitches. Gauge is not as important when crocheting an afghan or purse, but it is critical when making clothing. You do not want a garment meant for an adult to end up fitting a five-year-old. It can easily happen.

Work up a 4" × 4" (10cm × 10cm) swatch of your chosen yarn before beginning any garment, measuring the gauge in the center of the swatch. To do that, place straight pins at the beginning and end of the designated measurement(s) or number of stitches in the gauge, and then count the number of stitches between the pins. If you want your item to fit or to look like the one in the project photo, your gauge must match the gauge given with the pattern. If your gauge does not match the gauge listed, keep trying with a larger or smaller hook until you get the correct gauge. Check your garment often, because when you set it aside and come back later, your gauge could be quite different. It happens to everyone. They say that when we are stressed, we tend to crochet tighter, and I can attest to that!

Something you need to know before starting any pattern in this book is that I tend to crochet looser than most people, so you may need to use a larger hook than what the patterns call for.

getting the right gauge

Measure your gauge carefully before beginning your project, and check it periodically on your garment as you work to ensure it will turn out as intended.

INCHES 1 2 3

605-P

PICAS
(6 & 12 PT.)   6   8   10   12   14   16   18
        1 2 3 4 5   7   9   11   13   15   17   19

choosing your yarn or thread

Weight refers to yarn thickness. The thicker the yarn, the larger the stitches you can make. Thicker yarn also requires a larger hook. Although most smaller-weight yarn labels suggest a smaller hook, I've shown in this book how pairing a larger hook with a smaller yarn creates a soft, drapeable fabric that's more flattering. If a pattern calls for a chunky yarn, you can't expect the same results with a much thinner sport weight. But you can expect all worsted-weight yarns to create the same kind of fabric. These yarn weights correspond to the gauge, or the number of stitches per inch that result in your finished piece.

If the yarn a pattern calls for isn't available in your area and you don't order it online, try the substitutions listed with most of the patterns, or shop around for other possibilities. Always crochet a swatch with the alternate yarn to make sure your gauge matches that of the original yarn. It may take you a couple tries when deciding which hook to use with your yarn to get the proper gauge, but don't skip this very important step.

how to change yarn color

To change to a new color with or without ending off the yarn, leave the last two loops on the last stitch of the old color on the hook. Pull the new color through both loops, and then continue with the pattern and the new color.

standard yarn weight system

yarn weight symbol and category names	types of yarns in a category
SUPER FINE **1** SUPER FIN Super Fino	sock, fingering, baby
FINE **2** FIN Fino	sport, baby
LIGHT **3** LEGER Ligero	DK, light worsted
MEDIUM **4** MOYEN Medio	worsted, afghan, aran
BULKY **5** BULKY Abultado	chunky, craft, rug
SUPER BULKY **6** SUPER BULKY Super Abultado	bulky, roving

how graduated stitching works

In traditional crochet, the same stitch would be worked on the same row. For example, one garment might require that you work all double-crochet stitches on the same row. Then, you'd use increases or decreases to make the parts of that garment gradually wider or narrower. With my Graduated Stitch Method, however, instead of using increases and decreases to create fitted clothing and accessories, you can shape an item simply by placing short and tall stitches on the same row.

In this book, the instructions with each pattern tell you which stitches you'll use for that particular design. You will find that some of the patterns will have single-crochet stitches on the same row as double-crochet stitches, and sometimes even slip stitches on the same row as double crochets. The different stitch heights are what do all the shaping for you. Many of the projects will be worked with straight rows that go back and forth, but as you work the piece, you'll see it is not shaped with straight lines.

This method of crochet is rather addicting, especially when you find out how many things you can make you never thought possible. I am constantly coming up with new projects using this method, and I'm sure before long you will come up with some of your own.

important notes about the patterns

With one or two exceptions, graduated stitching is used with all the book's projects, but in addition to that, there are two other methods used to create some of the designs. I have used a combination of these three methods in the patterns, and this combination makes up the flattering outcome of each project.

Graduated Stitch Method. Working different stitch heights on the same row creates shaping that looks and acts like increases and decreases.

Side-to-side method. Because everyone's body shape is different, this method allows you to custom fit your garment to your own unique body by adding rows to or deleting rows from the basic instructions.

Back-loop-only method. Using the back loop only (blo) method—placing your hook in one loop instead of two—helps make garments that are stretchable and drapeable for a better fit and feel.

Many of the designs in this book will use the blo method. Traditionally, going in the blo has been used to create a ribbing on the cuffs, bottom and neck of sweaters, creating an elastic effect to give a snug fit in that area. On the garments or accessories that feature the blo technique, I show how you can work the ribbed section right into the piece, instead of having to make it separately and sew it on later. This saves time and frustration.

sizing information

I recommend circling the size you are making on each pattern for less confusion. If you go by the measurements listed in the pattern, the garment should fit. If you want a formfitted garment, try making one size smaller than your bust measurement. If you want a loose garment, make your actual size or perhaps one size larger than your bust measurement. Keep in mind when choosing the size you wish to make that most of these garments stretch to conform to the body. To determine the appropriate-sized poncho or capelet, measure around the arms, bust and back with the arms down at the sides.

dtr hdtr tr htr dc hdc sc sl st

comparing stitch heights

This diagram shows how crochet stitches gradually become taller, starting with the shorter slip stitch and ending with the taller double treble.

Working in the back loop really helps shape the body of a garment and is also a key part of crocheting pieces that will fit and conform to the body. When a piece is crocheted with stitches in the back loop, it will stretch. The stretching of the blo method will also help shape a piece. Because there is such a difference in measurements from the neck to the shoulders, such as with the basic capelet on page 24, working the double-crochet stitches in the back loops will make the double-crochet part stretch across the shoulders.

making crocheted garments drapeable

Knitting picks up only one loop at a time, which is why knitting is not as thick as crochet, therefore making knitted items more drapeable. Because working in the back loop only looks a lot like knitting, items crocheted in this way feel soft and drapeable as if they *were* knitted—especially if you use a larger hook than the one recommended

for a particular yarn and work looser stitches.

The size of the yarn and hook used is a major consideration in this book. For instance, for the open and delicate ruffled shrug on page 109 I used a very fine yarn with a much larger hook than is normally called for to construct it. The resulting soft piece is as light as a feather, unlike many crocheted items you may have seen before.

sewing seams

With the exception of a few garments, you will have to sew only one or two seams on most of the garments that use graduated stitching. Most of the garments are worked from side to side and are never worked in the round, even though it may appear that way. (The only exception is the houndstooth-check felted purse, which is worked in the round.) You will always have a side seam if you have a piece that looks circular, such as the capelet. Some of the designs, such as the wrap on page 59, do not require any seam at all.

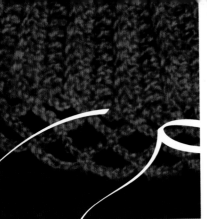

CHAPTER ONE

SIX DESIGNS *from* ONE BASIC PATTERN

With a few modifications, a simple capelet design can result in a number of beautiful endings, including a skirt, hat, poncho or purse. Each project will have its own set of instructions because the yarn, hooks and number of stitches used may vary. Most of these projects require using two hook sizes on the same row, as well as shorter and taller stitches to create the shaped effect shown. Don't be intimidated, though: All the projects are easy enough for a beginner.

where it all began
THE BASIC CAPELET PATTERN

One day I wanted to make a capelet that would have a smaller neck area. I personally do not mind crocheting things in the round, but some people are afraid to even try. I have taught many to crochet, so I am always trying to come up with easy ways my students can do things.

For this particular capelet, I had the idea to make a rectangle I could seam up on one side to look like it was crocheted in the round. I have known for years that working in the back loop will help cause a garment to stretch. I have studied knitting and what makes it drapeable. Knitting is less dense than crocheting because the needles catch only one loop. But in crochet stitches are formed by picking up two loops at a time, making the piece thicker or denser.

Traditionally, to get the shape of a capelet in the round, you would use one hook size, and you would have to start either at the bottom and decrease at the neck or start at the neck and increase as you work downward. But with my method of graduated stitching, you do not ever increase or decrease. Instead of starting at the neck and working the entire capelet in the round—increasing as you go—the smaller part that narrows at the top-neck section is done with a shorter single-crochet stitch and a smaller hook, causing it to narrow on its own. (See the basic capelet diagram on page 25.)

Changing the hook size on the same row emphasizes the difference in heights even more. After sewing the side seam, the piece may look too small, but when the piece is put on, it stretches to fit around the shoulders. As mentioned before, what makes the piece stretch is the fact that you are using the back-loop-only (blo) method when you crochet the rows.

The piece will have ridges. This is also called *ribbing* and is a pattern stitch normally used for sweater cuffs. Working in the back loop causes the piece to stretch even more, providing a fit that hugs the body.

Making a top or sweater this way, with vertical rows instead of horizontal rows, gives a flattering fit.

This is how I came up with the Graduated Stitch Method. I excitedly began to think of ways this method of using different stitch heights on the same row could shape and form other flattering garments. I looked at my basic capelet design and said, "What else can I do with this piece?" My imagination ran wild, and I came up with ten different projects based on this same capelet pattern. Some of those projects are featured on the following pages. Other projects I made from the basic capelet pattern are not shown in this book: a round pillow cover, a lamp shade, a felted bowl and a Christmas tree skirt. Perhaps those home décor items can be reserved for another book?

The projects on the following pages are all easy enough for beginners but enjoyable enough for the more experienced. If you've never made anything else in crochet before now, you'll find these projects to be very simple!

BULKY
5
BULKY
Abultado

1 BEGINNER

2 ADVANCED
  BEGINNER

3 INTERMEDIATE

This capelet pattern is incredibly versatile, as you will see in the projects to come. It has no increases or decreases, and you won't believe how easy it will be for you to make any of the five projects that follow based on this single pattern. You will be able to make any project in any size, custom fitting it to your body.

basic capelet

size

Fits sizes XSM (SM, MED, LG, XLG, 1X, 2X, 3X)

This same capelet can be made for all girls' sizes (from infant to girl's size 16) (see Pattern Notes). Sizes are determined by number of beg chs and rows worked.

Finished length (including scalloped rows on bottom edge): approx 12½" (32cm) long

Finished bottom width: approx 44" (46", 48", 50", 52", 54", 56", 58"); 112 (117, 122, 127, 132, 137, 142, 147) cm

materials

3 (3, 3, 3, 4, 4, 4, 4) skeins (2.8 oz/84 yd/80 g per skein) #5 bulky yarn

Used in this project: Patons Rumor alpaca-blend yarn in Hibiscus Heather (Substitutes: Moda Dea Swirl or Moda Dea Gleam)

Sizes K/10½ (6.5mm) and N/13 (9mm) crochet hooks

Yarn needle

Stitch marker

gauge

With K hook, 6 sc and 4 sc rows = 2" (5cm)

With N hook, 8 dc and 4 dc rows (at widest point) = 4" (10cm)

stitches used

ch, sc, dc, sl st

pattern notes

All sts are worked in the blo. Sts for the scalloped edging are worked in both lps. Rows are worked vertically from side to side, making it easy to add rows to fit body if needed. Beg ch will be at back seam. Two hook sizes are used on the same row.

For a longer capelet: Make beg ch longer and add to the number of dc on each row.

For larger than a size 3X: Work more rows to fit around shoulders, using the same basic capelet instructions. For a longer capelet, make beg ch longer and add to the number of dc on each row.

For all girls' sizes: Make your beg ch the length you want by holding it up to the wearer. Use the same basic capelet instructions, remembering that if you use a smaller yarn (and possibly smaller hooks), you may need to work more chs and sts on each row. Work as many rows needed to wrap around the shoulders.

basic capelet diagram

The finished piece will look like this before sewing the side seam. The sc and dc stitches will be on the same row, and you'll change your hook size.

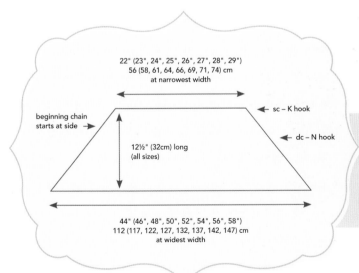

22" (23", 24", 25", 26", 27", 28", 29")
56 (58, 61, 64, 66, 69, 71, 74) cm
at narrowest width

beginning chain starts at side →

12½" (32cm) long
(all sizes)

← sc – K hook

← dc – N hook

44" (46", 48", 50", 52", 54", 56", 58")
112 (117, 122, 127, 132, 137, 142, 147) cm
at widest width

instructions

All sts are worked in the blo. With N hook, ch 15; change to K hook and ch 9 – 24 chs total. (For longer capelet: Add to the 15 chs here with N hook, for desired length. Then add same number of dc on each row.)

Row 1: (RS) With K hook, sc in 2nd ch from hook and in next 7 chs. Pm in last sc made (8 sc made will form the neck); change to N hook and dc in last 15 chs; turn – 23 sts. At this point, piece should measure approx 10" (25cm) long.

Row 2: With N hook, ch 3 (counts as first dc), sk first dc, dc in blo of next 14 dc. Take marker out of sc and place in last dc made; change to K hook and sc in blo of next 8 sc; turn – 15 dc and 8 sc (23 sts total).

Row 3: With K hook, ch 1, sc in blo of first 8 sc. Pm in last sc made. Change to N hook and dc in blo of next 14 dc, dc in 3rd ch of beg ch-3; turn – 23 sts.

Rows 4–44 (46, 48, 50, 52, 54, 56, 58): Rep rows 2 and 3 appropriate number of times, ending by working a Row 2 rep. For wider capelet: Add more rows (working an even number of rows if you plan to work scalloped edging); end off after last row. When lying flat, before seam is sewn, the basic capelet should measure approx 44" (46", 48", 50", 52", 54", 56", 58"); 112 (117, 122, 127, 132, 137, 142, 147) cm at the widest point (bottom) and approx 22" (23", 24", 25", 26", 27", 28", 29"); 56 (58, 61, 64, 66, 69, 71, 74) cm at the narrowest (top).

assembling capelet

With RS tog, match up sts on foundation ch and last row. Sew side seam with yarn and yarn needle.

scalloped edging

Worked in both lps.

Rnd 1: With RS facing and K hook, join with sl st in center of any dc row at wide end (bottom) of capelet. (Dc sts will be sideways – horizontal.); * ch 3, sl st in center of next horizontal dc; rep from * around entire capelet edge, ending with sl st in first sl st – total number of ch-3 sps will be same as total number of rows you worked on capelet. (Example: If you worked 48 rows, you will have 48 ch-3 sps.) Do not turn.

Rnd 2: Sl st in first 2 chs of next ch-3 sp, * ch 7, sk next ch-3 sp, sl st in next ch-3 sp; rep from * around, ending with sl st in first sl st – total number of ch-7 sps will be half the total of rows you worked. (Example: If you worked 48 rows on capelet, you will have 24 ch-7 sps.)

Rnds 3–4: Sl st in first 4 chs of next ch-7 sp; * ch 7, sl st in 4th ch of next ch-7 sp, rep from * around, ending with sl st in first sl st – same number of ch-7 as Rnd 2. End off after last rnd. Weave in loose ends.

SKILL LEVEL:

LIGHT
3
LEGER
Ligero

1 BEGINNER

2 ADVANCED
BEGINNER

3 INTERMEDIATE

The neck of the capelet becomes the waist on this pleated-look skirt. It can be made in any size from infant to adult 6X; all you have to do is lengthen or shorten the beginning chain. Make it as wide or narrow as needed by choosing the number of rows worked. A pretty, optional edging can be added to make it extra special.

short skirt

size

Fits toddler and girl sizes 1–2 (3–4, 5–6, 7–8, 8–10, 10–12, 12–14, 14–16)

This same skirt can be made for all women's sizes up to 6X (see Pattern Notes).

Finished length: approx 9" (10", 11", 12¼", 13¼", 14½", 15½", 16½"); 23 (25, 28, 31, 34, 37, 39, 42) cm

Finished waist: approx 16" (17", 18", 19", 20", 21", 22", 23"); 41 (43, 46, 48, 51, 53, 56, 58) cm

materials

1 (1, 1, 2, 2, 2, 3, 3) skeins (6 oz/330 yd) #3 light worsted-weight yarn

Used in this project: Caron Simply Soft acrylic yarn in Country Blue (Substitute: Red Heart Hula)

Sizes H/8 (5mm) and J/10 (6mm) crochet hooks

Yarn needle

Stitch marker

gauge

With H hook, 9 sc and 8 sc rows = 2" (5cm)

With J hook, 11 dc and 6 dc rows (at widest point) = 3" (8cm)

stitches used

ch, sl st, sc, dc

Special stitch: shell (for optional scalloped edging): (sc, hdc, 2 dc, hdc, sc) in ch-5 sp

pattern notes

This skirt has one seam in back. Beg ch will be length of skirt minus ½" (1cm). Rows are worked vertically, making it easy to add rows to fit the body if needed.

For all women's sizes, up to 6X: With J hook, make beg ch the length you desire the skirt to be. With H hook, sc into 2nd ch from hook and in next 10 chs (11 chs total for waist section). Change to J hook and work dc in rem chs. Follow rows 2 and 3 of girl's skirt instruction (blo, so it will stretch), replacing the number of dc with number of dc you worked into your beg ch on Row 1. Keep working until you have enough rows to fit around your body. Remember to work an even number of rows if you plan to work sps for drawstring and edging. End off and sew back seam. Weave in ends.

instructions

All sts are worked in the blo.

With J hook, ch 22 (26, 30, 34, 38, 42, 46, 50). For shorter or longer skirt: delete or add chs here, deleting or adding to the dc section at bottom of skirt. Change to H hook and ch 12 – 34 (38, 42, 46, 50, 54, 58, 62) chs.

Row 1: (RS) With H hook, sc in 2nd ch from hook and in next 10 chs (11 sc made). Pm in last sc made; change to J hook, dc in next 22 (26, 30, 34, 38, 42, 46, 50) chs; turn – 33 (37, 41, 45, 49, 53, 57, 61) sts.

Row 2: With J hook, ch 3 (counts as first dc), sk first dc, dc in blo of next 21 (25, 29, 33, 37, 41, 45, 49) dc. Take marker out of sc and place in last dc made; change to H hook, sc in blo of next 11 sc; turn – 33 (37, 41, 45, 49, 53, 57, 61) sts.

Row 3: With H hook, ch 1, sc in blo of first 11 sc. Take marker out of dc and place in last sc made; change to J hook, dc in blo of next 22 (26, 30, 34, 38, 42, 46, 50) dc, ending with last dc in 3rd ch of beg ch-3; turn – 33 (37, 41, 45, 49, 53, 57, 61) sts.

Rows 4–64 (68, 72, 76, 80, 84, 88, 92) or to desired width: Rep rows 2 and 3 appropriate number of times, ending by working a Row 2 rep. End off after last row. Weave in ends. When lying flat, before seam is sewn, the skirt should measure approx 16" (17", 18", 19", 20", 21", 22", 23"); 41 (43, 46, 48, 51, 53, 56, 58) cm at narrowest point (top waist) and approx 32" (34", 36", 38", 40", 42", 44", 46"); 81 (86, 91, 97, 102, 107, 112, 117) cm at widest point (bottom). With RS tog, match up foundation ch and last row. Sew seam with yarn and yarn needle. Turn RS out.

drawstring waist

With RS facing and H hook, join yarn with sl st in top center back edge at seam; ch 5 (counts as first dc and ch-2 sp); * sk next row, dc in edge of next row, ch 2; rep from * around, ending with sl st in 3rd ch of beg ch-5. End off. – 32 (34, 36, 38, 40, 42, 44, 46) dc and 32 (34, 36, 38, 40, 42, 44, 46) ch-2 sps. If you added or deleted rows on your skirt: The number of dc and ch-2 sps will be half the number of rows you worked. (Example: 66 rows = 33 dc and 33 ch-2 sps.)

drawstring

Ch 170. End off. Weave drawstring or ribbon through ch-2 sps, beg at center front. Weave in ends.

optional scalloped edging (not shown)

Rnd 1: With RS facing and H hook, join yarn with sl st in top edge of any dc row at bottom edge of skirt; * ch 5, sk next row, sl st in top edge of next row; rep from * around, ending with sl st in joining sl st – 32 (34, 36, 38, 40, 42, 44, 46) ch-5 sps.

Rnd 2: Ch 1, * shell in next ch-5 sp, sl st in next sl st; rep from * around, ending with sl st in joining sl st. End off. – 32 (34, 36, 38, 40, 42, 44, 46) shells. Weave in loose ends.

for less bulk

A lighter-weight yarn will make your skirt less bulky, but realize you may need to use smaller hooks, and your gauge will change.

SKILL LEVEL:

MEDIUM
4
MOYEN
Medio

1 **BEGINNER**

2 ADVANCED
BEGINNER

3 INTERMEDIATE

If you like turtlenecks, this is the capelet for you. The neck combined with the navy tweed yarn make it a perfect addition to your fall or winter wardrobe. It may appear small once finished, but remember that it stretches around the shoulders. The quick and easy arm warmers (see page 32) really add to this chic set. Make them longer or shorter, depending on the style you want.

turtleneck capelet *with* arm warmers

turtleneck capelet

size

Fits sizes XSM (SM, MED, LG, XLG, 1X, 2X, 3X)

This same capelet can be made for smaller girls or larger women's sizes (see Pattern Notes).

Finished length: approx 13" (33cm)

Finished bottom width: approx 40¾" (42", 43¼", 44¾", 46", 47¼", 48¾", 50"); 104 (107, 110, 114, 117, 120, 124, 127) cm

materials

2 (2, 2, 2, 3, 3, 3, 3) skeins (100 g/210 yd per skein) #4 medium worsted-weight yarn

Used in this project: Plymouth Galway Colornep wool blend yarn in Navy Blue (Substitutes: Plymouth Tweed or Caron Simply Soft Tweed)

Sizes K/10.5 (6.5mm) and G/6 (4mm) crochet hooks

Yarn needle

gauge

With G hook, 9 sc and 8 sc rows = 2" (5cm)

With K hook, 13 dc and 6 dc rows (at widest point) = 4" (10cm)

stitches used

ch, sc, dc

pattern notes

Two hook sizes are used on the same row. Rows are worked vertically, making it easy to add rows to fit the body if needed.

For a higher turtleneck: Make beg ch longer and work more sc in that area on each row.

For a longer capelet: Make beg ch longer and add to the number of dc on each row.

For smaller girls' or larger women's sizes: See the basic capelet Pattern Notes on page 25.

instructions

All sts are worked in the blo.

With K hook, ch 25, change to G hook and ch 23 – 48 chs.

Row 1: With G hook, sc in 2nd ch from hook and in next 21 chs (22 sc made will form the turtleneck); change to K hook and dc in next 25 chs; turn – 47 sts.

Row 2: With K hook, ch 3 (counts as first dc), sk first dc, dc in blo of next 24 dc (25 dc made); change to G hook and sc in blo of next 22 sc; turn – 47 sts.

Row 3: With G hook, ch 1, sc in blo of first 22 sc; change to K hook and dc in blo of next 25 dc, ending with last dc in 3rd ch of beg ch-3; turn – 47 sts.

Rows 4–61 (63, 65, 67, 69, 71, 73, 75) or to desired width: Rep rows 2 and 3 appropriate number of times. End off after last row. When lying flat, before side seam is sewn, this capelet should measure approx 40¾" (42", 43¼", 44¾", 46", 47¼", 48¾", 50"); 104 (107, 110, 114, 117, 120, 124, 127) cm at the widest point (bottom) and approx 15¼" (15¾", 16¼", 16¾", 17¼", 17¾", 18¼", 18¾"); 39 (40, 41, 43, 44, 45, 46, 48) cm at the narrowest point (top neck). Fold piece in half. Match up foundation ch and sts on last row. Sew up side seam. Fold down narrow top edge of capelet, forming turtleneck. Weave in ends.

arm warmers

size

One size fits most.

Finished length: 15" (38cm)

materials

1 skein (100 g/210 yd) #4 medium worsted-weight yarn

Used in this project: Plymouth Galway Colornep wool blend yarn in Navy Blue (Substitutes: Plymouth Tweed or Caron Simply Soft Tweed)

Size J/10 (6mm) crochet hook

Yarn needle

gauge

10 hdc and 6 hdc rows = 3" (8cm)

stitches used

ch, hdc

pattern notes

For shorter wrist warmers: Work less chs at beg for desired length.

For wider (larger) or smaller (child's sizes) arm warmers: Work more or less rows.

instructions

Make 2.

All sts are worked in the blo.

Ch 52.

Row 1: Hdc in 3rd ch from hook, hdc in each rem ch across; turn – 51 hdc (skipped chs count as first hdc).

Row 2: Ch 2 (counts as first hdc), sk first hdc, hdc in blo of next hdc and in blo of each hdc across, ending with last hdc in first skipped ch on Row 1; turn – 51 hdc.

Row 3: Ch 2 (counts as first hdc), sk first hdc, hdc in blo of next hdc and in blo of each hdc across, ending with last hdc in 2nd ch of beg ch-2; turn – 51 hdc.

Rows 4–16: Rep Row 3, 13 times more.

Row 17: Ch 2, sk first hdc, hdc in blo of next 44 hdc, ch 2 loosely, skip next 2 sts (for thumb hole), hdc in blo of last 4 hdc, ending with last hdc in 2nd ch of beg ch-2 – 49 hdc and 1 ch-2 sp for thumb hole. End off. Fold piece in half, matching up foundation ch and sts on last row. Sew side seam with yarn needle. Weave in ends.

BULKY
5
BULKY
Abultado

This poncho pattern is virtually the same as the adult capelet. You can make it adult or infant-sized by adding or deleting chains at the beginning and by working more or less rows to get the width you want. The pom-poms are a fun touch, but you could replace them with beaded fringe worked around the entire edge.

pom-pom poncho

size

Fits girl sizes 1–2 (3–4, 5–6, 7–8, 10–12, 12–14)

This same poncho can be made for an adult (see Pattern Notes). Sizes are determined by number of beg chs and rows worked.

Finished length: approx 11" (28cm) plus 2" (5cm) pom-poms

Finished bottom width: approx 33¼" (35", 36¾", 38¼", 40", 41¾"); 84 (89, 93, 97, 102, 106) cm

materials

3 (3, 3, 4, 4, 4) skeins (5 oz/140 g/255 yd per skein) #5 bulky yarn

Used in this project: Bernat bouclé yarn in Soft Rose (Substitute: Lion Brand bouclé)

Sizes H/8 (5mm) and K/10.5 (6.5mm) crochet hooks

1 pack Pink Pony beads with large holes

Yarn needle

Stitch marker

gauge

With H hook, 7 sc and 5 sc rows = 2" (5cm)

With K hook, 10 dc = 4" (10cm); 3 dc rows (at widest point) = 2½" (6cm)

All sizes: If you use a smaller or larger yarn than what the pattern calls for, your gauge will change from the gauge listed here.

stitches used

ch, sc, dc

pattern notes

Two hook sizes are used on the same row. Rows are worked vertically from side to side, making it easy to add rows to fit the body if needed. Beg ch will be at side seam.

For a longer poncho: Make beg ch longer and add to the number of dc on each row.

To make an adult-sized poncho: Work more rows to fit around the shoulders, using the same basic poncho instructions. If a longer poncho is desired, work a longer beg ch and add dc to the number of dc listed.

instructions

All sts are worked in the blo.

With K hook, ch 20; change to H hook and ch 11 – 31 chs total. (For longer poncho: Add to the 20 beg chs here with size K hook to desired length. Then add same number of dc on each row.)

Row 1: With H hook, sc in 2nd ch from hook and in next 9 chs. Pm in last sc made (10 sc made will form the neck); change to K hook and dc in last 20 chs; turn – 30 sts. Note: At this point, piece should measure approx 11" (28cm) long.

Row 2: With K hook, ch 3 (counts as first dc), sk first dc, dc in blo of next 19 dc. Take marker out of sc and place in last dc made; change to H hook and sc in blo of next 10 sc; turn – 20 dc and 10 sc (30 sts total).

Row 3: With H hook, ch 1, sc in blo of first 10 sc. Take marker out of dc and place in last sc made; change to K hook and dc in blo of next 20 dc, ending with last dc in 3rd ch of beg ch-3; turn – 30 sts.

Rows 4–40 (42, 44, 46, 48, 50): Cont working in patt, rep rows 2 and 3 appropriate number of times and ending by working a Row 2 rep. For wider poncho: Add more rows, making sure you work an even number of rows if you plan to add pom-poms and fringe, so they will be evenly spaced around. End off after last row. When lying flat, before side seam is sewn, this poncho should measure approx 33¼" (35", 36¾", 38¼", 40", 41¾"); 84 (89, 93, 97, 102, 106) cm at the widest point (bottom) and approx 16" (16¾", 17½", 18½", 19¼", 20"); 41 (43, 44, 47, 49, 51) cm at the narrowest point (top neck).

With RS tog, match up foundation chs and sts on last row. Sew side seam with yarn and yarn needle.

pom-poms

Each pom-pom is approx 2" (5cm) in diameter.

You can use a pom-pom maker, or follow this simple method: Cut a ¾" (2cm) piece of cardboard. Wind the yarn around the cardboard approx 105 times. Cut a 12" (30cm) piece of yarn and slip it through the lps. (Note: Use a plain piece of pink yarn with the bouclé because the bouclé yarn tends to break easily.) Tie the yarn securely so it will not come loose. Slip the lps off the cardboard. Cut the lps on the untied end and fluff out the pom-pom. Trim to desired size.

Tie pom-poms evenly spaced around bottom edge of poncho (approx every 3–4 rows).

fringe

Cut 6"–7" (15–18cm) strands of yarn for fringe. The number you cut will depend on the number you place between each pom-pom. Take 1–2 strands to place between each pom-pom, folding the strand so one will be longer than the other. Place a bead on the end of each strand and tie a knot to secure. Rep this around entire the poncho. Weave in the ends.

SKILL LEVEL:

MEDIUM
4
MOYEN
Medio

1 BEGINNER

2 ADVANCED
BEGINNER

3 INTERMEDIATE

The neck edge on the basic capelet pattern becomes the crown of this unisex hat, which can be made in any size for a child or adult—even for a doll! Try using textured yarn for a different look. The braids are fun, but you could attach a pom-pom just as easily. Work shorter rows for a beanie or skullcap.

toboggan hat

size

Fits all sizes, depending on number of rows worked. Hat shown will fit a child; is approx 7½" (19cm) long with 2" (5cm) brim folded up x 17" (43cm) circumference.

materials

1 hank (4 oz/375 yd per hank) #4 medium worsted-weight yarn in multicolor blues, purples and greens

Used in this project: Handpainted Sock-ezze 75% Superwash wool and 24% nylon yarn (from www.yarnsmiths.com) (Substitute: Red Heart TLC Essentials)

Sizes H/8 (5mm) and I/9 (5.5mm) crochet hooks

Yarn needle

gauge

With H hook, 8 sc and 6 sc rows = 2" (5cm)

With I hook, 13 dc and 6 dc rows = 3" (8cm)

stitches used

ch, sc, dc

pattern notes

Beg ch will be at side seam. The entire hat is worked in the blo, which causes the hat to stretch and gives a textured ridge.

For a shorter hat or infant size: Work less chs at beg for a shorter hat, and work less rows to fit around any size infant head.

For a larger adult size: Work more chs at beg to get the length you want with the turned-up edge, and work more rows to custom fit around head.

For an 18" (46cm) doll: With H hook ch 16, with F/5 (3.75mm) hook ch 5 – 21 chs. Work doll hat using the basic hat instructions, with 4 sc and 16 dc in each row for a total of 20 sts in each row, working enough rows to fit around the doll's head (approx 23 rows). Add a pom-pom to the crown, if desired.

instructions

All sts are worked in the blo.

With H hook, ch 42.

Row 1: (RS) sc in 2nd ch from hook and in next 10 chs; change to I hook, dc in next 30 chs; turn – 11 sc and 30 dc (41 sts).

Row 2: With I hook, ch 3 (counts as first dc), sk first dc, dc in blo of next 29 dc; change to H hook, sc in blo of next 11 sc; turn – 30 dc and 11 sc (41 sts).

Row 3: With H hook, ch 1, sc in blo of first 11 sc; change to I hook, dc in blo of next 30 dc, ending with last dc in 3rd ch of beg ch-3; turn – 11 sc and 30 dc (41 sts).

Rows 4–34: Rep rows 2 and 3, 15 times more, then rep Row 2 once more. End off after last row, leaving a 10" (25cm) tail. With RS tog, match up foundation chs and sts on last row. Pin in place. Sew side seam. With 10" (25cm) tail and yarn needle, gather narrow top edge (sc end) to close up crown. Tie ends of yarn to secure. Turn RS out and fold up bottom edge.

braids

Approx 9" (23cm) long.

Wind yarn around a 12" (30cm) piece of cardboard 41 times (the same way you'd make a tassel). Cut a 12" (30cm) piece of yarn and slip it through top lps. Tie the yarn securely so it will not come loose. Cut ends at bottom and take off cardboard. Wrap yarn around the folded yarn at top, about ½" (1cm) down from the top and secure (as you would a tassel). Sepa-rate the 81 strands into 3 sets of 27 strands each, and braid each one. (Each braid should have 3 sets of 9 strands each.) Secure end of each braid by wrapping yarn around strands approx 2" (5cm) from end and secure by tying a knot. You can tie a bow with yarn or ribbon here.

Place braids on RS of crown. Attach to hat by weaving the loose ends at tops of braids into inside of crown and secure. Weave in ends.

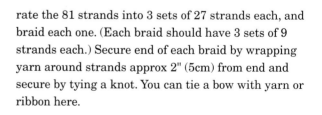

MEDIUM
4
MOYEN
Medio

1 BEGINNER

2 ADVANCED
BEGINNER

3 INTERMEDIATE

The neck of the basic capelet becomes the gathered bottom of this bag. You could even choose to gather the bottom of the capelet and use the neck opening at the top. It has a crocheted handle that can be tucked inside the purse when you'd rather attach a leather strap. Instructions are also given for a crochet chain drawstring, but a pretty ribbon can look more formal. Dress up the bag as much as you want with beads, fringe or a tassel on the bottom.

hobo bag

size

Approx 9" (23cm) high x 7" (18cm) wide
(without strap)

materials

2 balls (100 g/135 yd per ball) #4 medium
worsted-weight yarn

Used in this project: Reynolds Cabana cotton
blend yarn in Plum (Substitutes: TLC Cotton Plus
or Lion Brand Cotton)

Sizes I/9 (5.5mm) and F/5 (3.75mm) crochet
hooks

1 yd (91cm) of ½" (1cm) wide satin ribbon
(optional)

2 wooden beads (with hole large enough
for yarn and needle to go through)

Yarn needle

Stitch marker

Any length leather strap with latch hooks
on each end (optional)

gauge

With I hook, 13 dc and 6 dc rows =
3½" (9cm)

stitches used

ch, sl st, sc, dc

pattern notes

You can make the bag in the same manner as
the capelet, with the same size yarn and same
hook sizes, but it will be big. To make it smaller
and firmer, use a smaller, stiffer yarn and smaller
hooks. Just as with the capelet, this purse is
worked from side to side, and the beg ch will be
your side seam.

For a smaller bag: Shorten your beg ch and
work less rows (in multiples of 6 for top edging
to work evenly).

instructions

All sts are worked in the blo.

With size I hook, ch 29; change to F hook, ch 6 – 35 chs total.

Row 1: (WS) With F hook, sc in 2nd ch from hook and in next 4 chs (5 sc made); change to I hook and dc in last 29 chs; turn – 34 sts.

Row 2: (RS) With I hook, ch 3 (counts as first dc), sk first dc, dc in blo of next 28 dc; change to F hook and sc in blo of next 5 sc; turn – 29 dc and 5 sc (34 sts total).

Row 3: With F hook, ch 1, sc in blo of first 5 sc; change to I hook and dc in blo of next 29 dc, ending with last dc in 3rd ch of beg ch-3; turn – 34 sts.

Rows 4–36: Rep rows 2 and 3, 16 times more, ending by working a Row 2 rep; do not end off.

to assemble bag

With RS tog, match up sts on foundation ch and last row. Place pins along seam edge to hold in place. Using I hook, loosely sl st in each st across rows through both thicknesses, starting at sc (bottom) end and working toward dc (top) end; do not end off. Turn bag RS out.

top edging of bag

Rnd 1: With I hook, ch 5 (counts as dc and ch-2 sp), * dc in top of dc on next row, ch 2, dc in top of beg ch-3 on next row, ch 2; rep from * around, ending with dc in top of dc on next row, ch 2; sl st in 3rd ch of beg ch-5 – 36 dc and 36 ch-2 sps.

Rnd 2: Ch 3 (counts as dc), dc in next ch-2 sp; * dc in next dc, dc in next ch-2 sp; rep from * around; join with sl st in 3rd ch of beg ch-3 – 72 dc.

Rnd 3: Change to F hook; * ch 5, sk next 2 dc, sl st in next dc; rep from * around, ending with sl st in first sl st; end off – 24 ch-5 sps.

bottom of bag

Turn bag inside out. With yarn needle, weave yarn through sc around edge of circle and pull tightly to gather, closing up hole. Work a few more sts to secure and end off. Turn bag RS out.

drawstring chain

With F hook, ch 110. End off.

Weave chain or optional ribbon through ch-2 sps on Rnd 1 on top edging of bag; gather and tie in a bow to close. Place bead onto loose end of drawstring with yarn needle and push bead close to st. Tie 2 knots under bead, to hold in place. Insert end back through bead and weave into chain.

crocheted strap
(worked on inside of bag)

On inside of bag, below drawstring row, pm at each side where you want to place strap. Join yarn with sl st in st to right of marker. Ch 60, without twisting ch, join with sl st in other side of bag in st to right of second marker, sl st in st to left (where marker was placed). Turn and dc in each ch across, sl st in st on other side of bag next to st where yarn was joined. End off. Weave in ends.

CHAPTER TWO

BEYOND *the* BASICS

expand your wardrobe with seventeen more graduated-stitch projects, from a little black dress that fits like a glove to cute and cozy slippers. None of these designs are alike, with one exception: The cap-sleeve top is similar to the little black dress, only shorter.

SKILL LEVEL:

LIGHT
3
LEGER
Ligero

1 BEGINNER

2 ADVANCED
BEGINNER

3 INTERMEDIATE

This stunner is the one you saw on the cover—perfect for a night out. The yarn chosen for it is light and airy, and the dress stretches and molds to the body for a comfortable fit that flatters.

little black dress

before you begin
GETTING THE RIGHT FIT

When you think "little black dress," you probably imagine a flattering fit, right? Well, that's exactly what I have tried to achieve with this design. The basic pattern is easy to follow, but I've also given instructions on how you can custom fit this dress to flatter your own unique body shape. For instance, if you are larger or smaller busted than average, or have narrower or wider hips, I have come up with an easy way for even a beginner to get a custom fit.

The length of the dress shown comes to the top of the knee on a person who is 5'5" (165cm) tall. If you want your dress to be shorter or longer, all you have to do is make your beginning chain longer or shorter than specified (add to the beg chain of 132). Make sure you add the same number of dc to the dc section below the empire waist that you added to the beginning chain. If you need a wider dress for your particular figure, simply add more rows than designated.

All the stitches are worked in the back loop only (blo), so this dress will stretch and conform to the body for a curve-hugging fit. Another key to success with this pattern is using a smaller DK (#2) weight yarn and a larger hook than the size recommended for that yarn weight. This makes your garment nice and drapeable. These principles apply to *any* crochet garment, and once you catch on to this easy concept, you'll be able to make your own custom-fit tops and sweaters as well, using my Graduated Stitch Method.

As you can see in the diagram, this dress is made up of straight rows consisting of single, half-double, double- and triple-crochet stitches. These stitches are all worked on the same row, and the different heights of the stitches is what shapes the dress—not increases or decreases. This pattern is very easy to follow because you basically repeat Row 1. Placing markers at the beginning or end of each section (single, half-double, double and triple crochet on same row) will help you keep track of each section and will make counting so much easier.

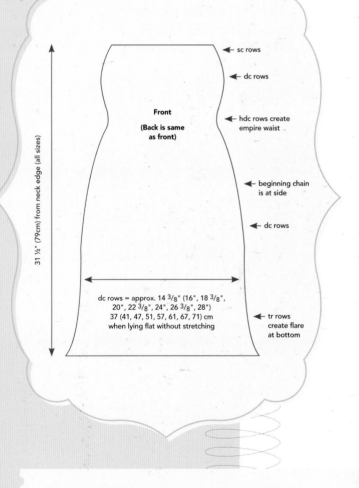

sc rows

dc rows

hdc rows create empire waist

Front
(Back is same as front)

beginning chain is at side

dc rows

31 ½" (79cm) from neck edge (all sizes)

dc rows = approx. 14 3/8" (16", 18 3/8", 20", 22 3/8", 24", 26 3/8", 28") 37 (41, 47, 51, 57, 61, 67, 71) cm when lying flat without stretching

tr rows create flare at bottom

little black dress diagram (without straps)

This is basically a rectangle, but it doesn't look that way, because the shorter single-crochet stitches on the same row shape the dress, making it look like you decreased. The taller triple-crochet stitches make it look like you increased on the bottom, but none of the patterns in this book have increases or decreases. Rows are worked vertically, from side to side, in the back loop only.

options

This pattern is so versatile, and there are many ways you can modify it to your taste.

You may want to make spaghetti straps instead of the straps shown in the photo. To make spaghetti straps, join the yarn with slip stitch in the desired stitch on the top edge of the front, chain the desired amount to go over the shoulder, and join with slip stitch in the desired stitch on the top edge of the back. Repeat in the desired stitches for the second strap.

You may want a closer fit under the bust (8 half-double crochet at the high waist). (See the cap-sleeve top on page 49.) You can either work all single crochet (instead of half double), or just work the half-double crochet in both loops, so it won't stretch as much there. You could also do the same with the single crochet at the neck edge (in both loops so it won't stretch). Or you could even use a smaller hook on the neck and waist.

You may not wish to have the bottom ruffle on your dress. If so, then work double-crochet stitches to the end of the row and just eliminate the triple-crochet stitches.

If you have a larger bust, you may not want to taper the half-double crochet stitches right below the bust. If you don't want to taper the stitches at the empire waist, simply work double-crochet stitches there instead of using the half doubles. Working more rows than the pattern calls for will also make that section (17 double crochet) larger to fit your bust.

easy does it

Because this is not an intricate stitch pattern, it's easy to watch TV or talk with a friend while working on this project.

using stitch markers

After working a few rows, you may not need the markers. But by using markers, you won't have to count the whole row at once. Counting each section (between markers) makes it much easier.

size

Fits sizes XSM (SM, MED, LG, XLG, 1X, 2X, 3X); size shown is XSM

All sizes: approx. 31" (79cm) long from neck edge to bottom edge (without straps).

Finished bust: approx. 28¾" (32", 36¾", 40", 44¾", 48", 52¾", 56"); 73 (81, 93, 102, 114, 122, 134, 143) cm

Note: See Sizing Information on page 18 to choose appropriate size.

materials

8 (10, 12, 14, 16, 18, 20, 22) balls (1.75 oz/166 yd/50 g each) #3 light worsted-weight yarn

Used in this project: Patons Brilliant yarn in Black Dazzle (Substitute: Nashua Grand Opera yarn)

Sizes F/5 (3.75mm) and G/6 (4mm) crochet hooks

Dritz Beading Elastic in black

Yarn needle

Stitch markers

gauge

With G hook:

7 sc = 1½" (4cm); 10 sc rows = 2½" (6cm)

8 hdc = 1¾" (4cm); 10 hdc rows = 3¼" (8cm)

17 dc = 4" (10cm); 10 dc rows = 4" (10cm)

10 tr = 2½" (6cm); 10 tr rows = 6" (15cm)

With F hook (on straps): 20 dc = 4" (10cm); 10 dc rows = 3½" (9cm)

stitches used

ch, sl st, sc, hdc, dc, tr

pattern notes

This dress is made to hit right above the knee on a 5'5" (165cm) tall person but can be made longer or shorter by adding or deleting chs at the beg. After you have worked the 2nd row, hold piece up to your body (from neck area, as in photo). Adjust beg ch if needed. Remember to add same amount of dc in dc section of row (add to the 86 dc) as chs added to beg ch. This dress is worked in 2 pieces from side to side. Straps are added after front and back are sewn tog. Elastic is crocheted onto top edge so straps will stay on shoulders. Rows on the dress are worked vertically, from side to side, in the blo. If you want your dress to be more form-fitting, delete rows or make it one size smaller.

instructions

All sts are worked in the blo.

front

All sizes: With G hook, loosely ch 132.

Row 1: Sc in 2nd ch from hook and in next 9 chs (10 sc made), pm in last sc made; dc in next 17 chs (for bust area), pm in last dc made; hdc in next 8 chs (for empire waist), pm in last hdc made; dc in next 86 chs, pm in last dc made; tr in next 10 chs (for flare at bottom of dress); turn – 131 sts.

Row 2: Ch 4 (counts as first tr), sk first tr, tr in blo of next 9 tr, take marker out of dc and place in last tr made; dc in blo of next 86 dc, take marker out of hdc and place in last dc made; hdc in blo of next 8 hdc, take marker out of dc and place in last hdc made; dc in blo of next 17 dc, take marker out of sc and place in last dc made; sc in blo of next 10 sc; turn – 131 sts.

Row 3: Ch 1, sc in blo of first 10 sc, take marker out of dc and place in last sc made; dc in blo of next 17 dc, take marker out of hdc and place in last dc made; hdc in blo of next 8 hdc, take marker out of dc and place in last hdc made; dc in blo of next 86 dc, take marker out of tr and place in last dc made; tr in blo of next 10 tr, ending with last tr in 4th ch of beg ch-4; turn – 131 sts.

Rows 4–36 (40, 46, 50, 56, 60, 66, 70): Rep rows 2 and 3 for desired width, ending by working a Row 2 rep. End off after last row.

Note: The piece may look small, but keep in mind that it stretches, so once the side seams are sewn, the dress should fit, according to the size you are making. If piece does not fit around the front of your body, you may need to add more rows.

back

Work same as front. With RS tog, match up sts at sides and pin in place. Sew seams with yarn and yarn needle, starting at bottom edge, leaving last 4"–4½" (10–11cm) open for armhole opening (forming a "V"). You can adjust the armhole opening later, if needed.

straps

Make 2.

All sts are worked in the (blo).

With F hook, ch 45 to measure approx. 8" (20cm), without stretching.

Note: After you have worked 2 rows, place strap at the shoulder to make sure it is long enough for your body. You may have to adjust the beg ch and number of dc in each row.

Row 1: Dc in 4th ch from hook (skipped chs count as first dc), dc in each rem ch across; turn – 43 dc.

Row 2: Ch 3 (counts as first dc), sk first dc, dc in blo of each dc across, ending with last dc in first skipped ch; turn – 43 dc.

Row 3: Work same as Row 2, ending with last dc in 3rd ch of beg ch-3.

Rows 4–10: Rep Row 3, 7 times more. End off after last row.

attaching straps to dress

Gather short ends of strap with yarn and yarn needle to measure approx. 2" (5cm) wide (or the width of sc section at top of dress, above bust area). Secure yarn with knot so it will stay in place. With RS tog, match up gathered ends of strap with the side edge of top where the sc sts begin and end. (See diagram for attaching straps on page 53.) Pin in place. Sew each end of strap to opening at side seam (on front and back). Rep on other side of dress. Placing strap here will allow you to wear straps at the shoulder, or you can wear straps off the shoulders by pushing them down a little.

adding elastic to neck edge

Beg in back, tie black elastic to any st on neck edge, leaving a 3" (8cm) tail. With RS facing and F hook, join yarn with sl st in same st as elastic, work sc evenly spaced around entire neck edge, encasing elastic between dress and sc sts; join with sl st in first sl st. Try on dress and adjust elastic to fit. End off yarn and secure elastic with knot. Weave in ends.

If needed, add elastic to bottom edge of straps in same manner. Weave in ends.

SKILL LEVEL:

LIGHT
3
LEGER
Ligero

1 BEGINNER

2 ADVANCED
BEGINNER

3 INTERMEDIATE

Wear this attractive top with a skirt for an elegant look, or go casual and pair it with jeans. Lengthen the design by adding to the double-crochet stitches below the empire waist, and you have a dress! The shiny threads in the yarn used here add a special touch.

cap-sleeve top

size

Fits sizes XSM (SM, MED, LG, XLG, 1X, 2X, 3X)

Finished length: approx 21" (53cm) from shoulder to bottom edge

Finished bust: 30" (34", 38", 42", 46", 50", 54", 58"); 76 (86, 97, 107, 117, 127, 137, 147) cm

Note: See Sizing Information on page 18 to choose appropriate size.

materials

5 (5, 6, 7, 8, 9, 10, 11) balls (1.75 oz/128 yd/50 g each) any #3 light worsted-weight yarn

Used in this project: Nashua Grand Opera yarn in Faded Lavender (Substitute: Patons Brilliant yarn)

Size F/5 (3.75 mm) crochet hook

Dritz Beading Elastic in black

Yarn needle

Stitch markers

gauge

6 sc and 4 sc rows = 1" (3cm)

18 dc and 8 dc rows = 4" (10cm) at widest point on dc rows

9 tr and 3 tr rows = 2" (5cm)

stitches used

ch, sl st, sc, hdc, dc, tr, picot, shell with picots

picot = ch 3, sl st in 3rd ch from hook

shell with picots = [hdc, picot (dc, picot) 3 times, hdc] in specified st or sp

pattern notes

This top is made similar to the little black dress on page 44, so read the notes on the dress before starting. It can be lengthened or shortened by adding or deleting chs at the beg. After you have worked the 2nd row, check to see if the top is the length you want. Be sure to place the piece up to area of your neck, as it shows in the photo. This would be the time to adjust your beg ch. It does not matter how many chs you add; just remember to add the same amount of dc in dc section of row (29 dc on front or 58 dc on back). If you do not want a fitted empire waist, work dc or hdc in place of sc on front under the bust area. This top is worked in two pieces from side to side, with a seam on each side. Straps are worked and then added separately after the front and back are sewn together.

For a longer top: Because 18 dc measure 4" (10cm), add 9 chs at beg and 9 more dc on each row per 2" (5cm).

For a fuller bust: Add to the bust area, if needed, in the 20 dc, placed over the fullest part. Add same number of chs and dc on back.

instructions

Sts are worked in the blo of front and back; sts are worked in both lps on shell edging.

front

Ch 80.

Row 1: (WS) Working in back bar of chs, sc in 2nd ch from hook and in next 9 chs, pm in last sc made; dc in next 20 chs (for bust area), pm in last dc made; sc in next 8 chs, creating a fitted empire waist; hdc in next ch, pm in hdc just made; dc in next 29 chs, pm in last dc made, tr in next 11 chs, creating flare at bottom; turn – 79 sts.

Row 2: (RS) Ch 4 (counts as first tr), sk first tr, tr in blo of next 10 tr, take marker out of dc and place in last tr made; dc in blo of next 29 dc; hdc in blo of next hdc, take marker out of hdc on previous row and place in hdc just made; sc in blo of next 8 sc, take marker out of dc and place in last sc made; dc in blo of next 20 dc, take marker out of sc and place in last dc made; sc in blo of next 10 sc; turn – 79 sts.

The top at this point should measure approx 16½" (42cm) long.

As mentioned in the Pattern Notes, this would be the time to make fitting adjustments in the beg ch to add to the length or the bust.

Row 3: Ch 1; sc in blo of first 10 sc, take marker out of dc and place in last sc made; dc in blo of next 20 dc; take marker out of sc and place in last dc made; sc in blo of next 8 sc; hdc in blo of next hdc, take marker out of hdc on previous row and place in hdc just made; dc in blo of next 29 dc, take marker out of tr and place in last dc made; tr in blo of next 11 tr, ending with last tr in 4th ch of beg ch-4; turn – 79 sts.

Note: After working a few rows, you may not need the stitch markers.

Rows 4–30 (34, 38, 42, 46, 50, 54, 58): Rep rows 2 and 3 for desired width, ending by working a Row 2 rep. End off after last row.

Note: If piece does not fit around front of body, you may need to add more rows. To add more rows, add an even number of rows on front and back so shells on the edging and seams will come out right. Keep in mind that this top stretches, so once the side seams are sewn, the top should fit according to the size you are making. Sizes are graded in increments of 2" (5cm) on front and 2" (5cm) on back, adding 4" (10cm) per size around.

cap-sleeve top diagram 1 (without straps)

The back is the same as the front but without the sc rows.

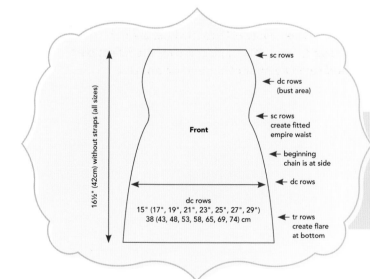

16½" (42cm) without straps (all sizes)

Front

← sc rows

← dc rows (bust area)

← sc rows create fitted empire waist

← beginning chain is at side

← dc rows

dc rows
15" (17", 19", 21", 23", 25", 27", 29")
38 (43, 48, 53, 58, 65, 69, 74) cm

← tr rows create flare at bottom

back

Work same as front, replacing the 8 sc under bust area with 8 dc. Work back sts as follows: (10 sc, 58 dc and 11 tr – on all rows – 79 sts). With RS tog, match up sts at sides and pin in place. Sew seams with yarn and yarn needle, starting at bottom edge, leaving last 4½"–5" (11–13cm) open for armhole opening (forming a "V"). You can adjust the armhole opening later after straps are added, if needed.

Note: This top is meant to be fitted. Add more rows (even number) for a looser fit.

straps

Make 2. All sts are worked in the blo.

Ch 41 (41, 41, 41, 45, 45, 45, 45).

Row 1: (RS) Dc in 4th ch from hook (skipped chs count as first dc), dc in each rem ch across; turn – 39 (39, 39, 39, 43, 43, 43, 43) dc.

Row 2: Ch 3 (counts as first dc), sk first dc, dc in blo of each dc across, ending with last dc in first skipped ch; turn – 39 (39, 39, 39, 43, 43, 43, 43) dc.

Row 3: Work same as Row 2, ending with last dc in 3rd ch of beg ch-3.

Rows 4–10: Rep Row 3, 7 times more. End off after last row. Strap should measure approx 8½" (8½", 8½", 8½", 9½", 9½", 9½", 9½") × 4½"; 22 (22, 22, 22, 24, 24, 24, 24) cm × 11cm.

attaching straps to top

Gather short ends of strap with yarn and yarn needle to measure approx 2½" (6.4cm). Secure yarn with knot so it will stay in place. With RS tog, place strap at top edge of each armhole opening on front and back at "V" with Row 1 at top of armhole opening and pin in place (see diagram on page 53). Sew strap with yarn and yarn needle. Placing strap here will allow you to wear straps at the shoulder, or you can wear straps off the shoulders by pushing them down a little. Rep on other side of top. Turn top RS out.

shell edging for straps

Right strap: With RS of right strap facing and top upside down, join yarn with sl st in first unjoined st on back armhole opening next to Row 10 of strap.

Row 1: * Ch 5, sk next 3 sts on strap, sl st in next st; rep from * across, ending with last sl st in next st on front armhole opening; turn – 10 (10, 10, 10, 11, 11, 11, 11) ch-5 sps.

Row 2: Ch 1, sc in first ch-5 sp; * ch 5, sc in next ch-5 sp; rep from * across; ch 3, join with sl st in next st on armhole opening; turn – 9 (9, 9, 9, 10, 10, 10, 10) ch-5 sps.

Row 3: Ch 1, sc in ch-3 sp; * shell with picots in next ch-5 sp, sc in next ch-5 sp; rep from * across. Sizes XSM–LG will end with a shell in last ch-5 lp, sl st in next st on armhole opening. Sizes XLG–3X will end with a sl st in last ch-5 lp. End off – 5 shells.

1 shell with picots = (1 hdc, picot, 1 dc, picot, 1 dc, picot, 1 dc, picot, 1 hdc)

Left strap: With WS of left strap facing and top upside down, join yarn with sl st in first unjoined st on back armhole opening next to Row 10 of strap. Work rows 1–3 same as right strap edging.

bottom shell edging

Row 1: With RS facing, join yarn to center of any tr st at bottom of back; * ch 5, sl st in center ch of next ch-4 (which counts as a tr st), ch 5, sl st in center of next tr; rep from * around entire bottom edge of top, working last sl st in first sl st – 60 (68, 76, 84, 92, 100, 108, 116) ch-5 sps. If you added or deleted vertical rows to top, number of ch-5 sps should be same as total number of rows on front and back tog.

Row 2: Sl st in next 2 chs, ch 1, sc in next ch; * ch 5, sc in next ch-5 sp; rep from * around, ending with sl st in first sc – 60 (68, 76, 84, 92, 100, 108, 116) ch-5 sps.

Row 3: Ch 1; work same as Row 3 of shell edging for straps, beg at first * around bottom edge of top. End with last sc in last ch-5 sp; join with sl st in first sl st. End off – 30 (34, 38, 42, 46, 50, 54, 58) shells. If you added or deleted vertical rows to top, number of shells should be half the total number of rows you worked on front and back tog.

adding elastic to neck edge

Beg in back, tie black elastic to any st on neck edge, leaving a 3" (8cm) tail. With RS facing, join yarn with sl st in same st as elastic, work sc evenly spaced around entire neck edge, encasing elastic between top and sc sts; sl st in first sl st. Try on top and adjust elastic to fit. End off yarn and secure elastic with knot. Weave in ends.

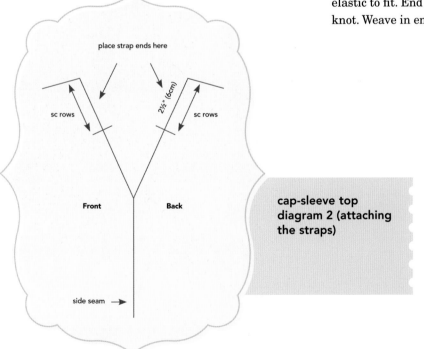

place strap ends here

2½" (6cm)

sc rows

sc rows

Front

Back

side seam →

cap-sleeve top diagram 2 (attaching the straps)

LIGHT
3
LEGER
Ligero

1 BEGINNER

2 ADVANCED BEGINNER

3 INTERMEDIATE

Fitted or loose? Long sleeves or short? This popular classic is all about options. Graduated stitching is used only at the neck area. Because this sweater is worked in the back loop only, it stretches, therefore allowing lots of ease. The decorative ribbon can be left off if you prefer a simpler look.

balletneck sweater

size

Fits sizes XSM (SM, MED, LG, XLG, 1X, 2X, 3X)
Note: See Sizing Information on page 18 to choose appropriate size.

Finished bust: 28" (32", 36", 40", 44", 48", 52", 56"); 71 (81, 91, 102, 112, 122, 132, 142) cm

materials

4 (4, 5, 5, 6, 6, 7, 7) skeins (3 oz/85 g/221 yd per skein) #3 light worsted-weight yarn

Used in this project: Bernat Satin Sport (Substitute: Lion Brand Microspun)

Size I/9 (5.5mm) crochet hook

1¼ yds (114cm) of ⅞" (2cm) wide satin ribbon

Yarn needle

Stitch markers

Aleene's OK To Wash-It glue (optional)

gauge

If you have more than 12 hdc to 3" (8cm), your sts are too tight, and you need to use a larger hook.

12 hdc and 9 hdc rows = 3" (8cm)
(blo sts and rows)

4 hdc and 4 hdc rows = 1⅛" (3cm) (sts in both lps: yoke and cuffs)

6 tr = 1¾" (4cm)

stitches used

ch, sl st, sc, hdc, tr

pattern notes

All sts except the yoke and cuffs are worked in the blo. The beg ch is at the side, and the sweater is worked from side to side. The top area of the sleeve is worked onto the armhole edge after the side seams are sewn. The piece for the bottom of the sleeve (the insert that is underneath) is worked separately, and rows are attached to the underarm opening as you go. Then the lower-sleeve insert is sewn to the upper-sleeve piece.

For a tighter fit: Make sweater one size smaller or delete rows in the front and back section.

For a longer top: Add to beg ch by adding 1 ch per hdc. 4 hdc per 1" (3cm) or 12 hdc per 3" (8cm). Be sure to add extra number of hdc to each row of pattern to avoid confusion.

For short sleeves: Instead of chaining 62 on Row 1 of sleeve, delete number of hdc by deleting chs (4 hdc per 1" [3cm], or 12 hdc per 3" [8cm].

instructions

All sts are worked in the blo.

front

All sizes: Loosely ch 48.

Row 1: (WS) hdc in 3rd ch from hook and in each rem ch across; turn – 46 hdc.

For XSM, SM, MED and LG only:

Row 2: (RS) Ch 2 (does not count as a st), hdc in

blo of each hdc across, ch 21 (armhole section); turn – 46 hdc and 21 chs. At this point, rows 1 and 2 (underarm rows) should measure approx 11½" (29cm) in length.

Row 3: (Beg of row is at neck edge.) Sc in 2nd ch from hook, hdc in next 19 chs (20 sts worked on ch), hdc in blo of next 46 hdc; turn – 66 sts (65 hdc and 1 sc).

Row 4: Ch 2 (does not count as a st), hdc in blo of each hdc, sc in blo of next sc; turn – 66 sts. Long rows should measure approx 16½" (42cm).

Row 5: Ch 1, sc in blo of first sc, hdc in blo of next 65 hdc; turn – 66 sts.

Rows 6–40 (46, 52, 58): Rep rows 4 and 5 appropriate number of times, ending by working a Row 4 rep. End off after last row.

Row 41 (47, 53, 59): This begins the first of 2 short rows at the side edge. With WS facing, beg at top neck edge, count over 20 sts and pm in 21st st. Join yarn with sl st in same st as marker, ch 2 (does not count as a st), hdc in blo of same st and in next 45 hdc; turn – 46 hdc.

Row 42 (48, 54, 60): Ch 2, hdc in blo of each hdc across. End off – 46 hdc.

For XLG and 1X only:

Rows 2–3: Ch 2 (does not count as a st), hdc in blo of each hdc across; turn – 46 hdc.

Rows 4–7: Work same as rows 2–5 on XSM.

Rows 8–62 (68): Rep rows 4 and 5 on XSM appropriate number of times, ending by working a Row 4 rep. End off after last row.

Rows 63 (69): Work same as Row 41 on XSM.

Rows 64–66 (70–72): Ch 2, hdc in blo of each hdc across; turn – 46 hdc. End off after last row.

For 2X and 3X only:

Rows 2–5: Ch 2 (does not count as a st), hdc in blo of each hdc across; turn – 46 hdc.

Rows 6–9: Work same as rows 2–5 on XSM.

Rows 10–72 (78): Rep rows 4 and 5 on XSM appropriate number of times, ending by working a Row 4 rep. End off after last row.

Row 73 (79): Work same as Row 41 on XSM.

Rows 74–78 (80–84): Ch 2, hdc in blo of each hdc across; turn – 46 hdc. End off after last row.

Note: First and last 2 (2, 2, 2, 4, 4, 6, 6) rows are short underarm rows.

back

Work same as front.

right seam

With RS tog, match up sts on first and last short rows. Pin in place. Sew seam at right of sweater with loose sl sts, catching both lps of each st in short row area. Left seam will be sewn later.

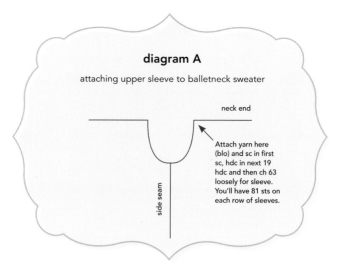

diagram A

attaching upper sleeve to balletneck sweater

neck end

Attach yarn here (blo) and sc in first sc, hdc in next 19 hdc and then ch 63 loosely for sleeve. You'll have 81 sts on each row of sleeves.

side seam

right sleeve

First 20 sts on Row 1 of upper sleeve will be crocheted onto side edge of armhole opening. With back of sweater on your lap and front facing, place sewn seam to your left and neck edge to your right.

Upper sleeve:

Row 1: With RS facing and working in free lps of chs at beg of first long row, join yarn with sl st in first ch (at neck edge at far right on front piece; see diagrams A on page 56 and B on page 57), ch 1, sc in same sp as joining, hdc in blo of next 19 sts, ch 63; turn – 1 sc, 19 hdc and 63 chs.

Row 2: Being careful not to twist ch, hdc in 3rd ch from hook (skipped chs do not count as a st), hdc in next 60 chs (61 hdc in ch), hdc in blo of next 19 hdc, sc in next sc; turn – 81 sts (80 hdc and 1 sc).

Row 3: Ch 1, sc in blo of first sc, hdc in blo of next 80 hdc; turn – 81 sts.

Row 4: Ch 2 (does not count as a st), hdc in blo of next 80 hdc, sc in blo of next sc; turn – 81 sts.

Rows 5–19 (21, 23, 23, 25, 25, 27, 29): Rep rows 3 and 4 appropriate number of times, ending by working a Row 3 rep. End off after last row – 81 sts on each row. Put sweater on and place upper sleeve around top and sides of your arm to determine if you need more or less rows. Remember you will have the added lower sleeve that will be sewn to upper sleeve (see diagram D on page 58).

Lower sleeve insert:

Lower sleeve will be sewn to upper sleeve later.

Row 1: With RS of short underarm rows facing, join yarn with sl st in top of last hdc on last short underarm row at underarm edge (see diagram C on page 57). Ch 63; turn. Hdc in 3rd ch from hook (skipped chs do not count as a st), hdc in next 60 chs, join with sl st in edge of underarm (short rows at beg and end of front and back that were seamed), sl st in edge of next row on underarm, ch 1; turn – 61 hdc.

Row 2: Hdc in blo of next 61 hdc; turn – 61 hdc.

Row 3: Ch 2 (does not count as a st), hdc in blo of next 61 hdc, join with sl st in edge of underarm, ch 1; turn – 61 hdc.

Row 4: Rep Row 2.

Row 5: Rep Row 3.

Row 6: Rep Row 2. Size XSM–MED – end off. Sizes LG–3X, keep repeating rows 3 and 2 until rows meet at other side edge of armhole, filling up the open space. This piece will hang loose.

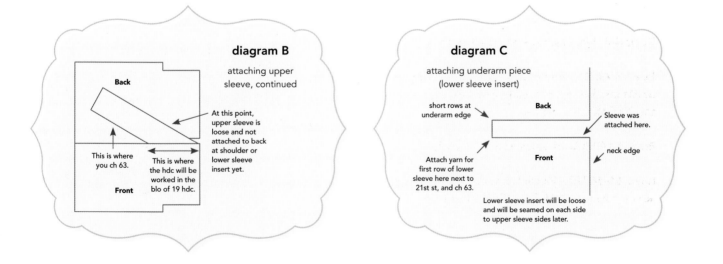

diagram B

attaching upper sleeve, continued

Back

At this point, upper sleeve is loose and not attached to back at shoulder or lower sleeve insert yet.

This is where you ch 63.

This is where the hdc will be worked in the blo of 19 hdc.

Front

diagram C

attaching underarm piece (lower sleeve insert)

short rows at underarm edge

Back

Sleeve was attached here.

Attach yarn for first row of lower sleeve here next to 21st st, and ch 63.

Front

neck edge

Lower sleeve insert will be loose and will be seamed on each side to upper sleeve sides later.

left seam and left sleeve

Sew left side seam of sweater same as right side seam. Turn sweater over so back is facing. Work left upper-sleeve piece and left underarm insert same as for the right sleeve.

Sew upper sleeve to lower sleeve: (Right sleeve) Turn sweater inside out. With RS tog, sew each side of lower sleeve to each side edge of upper sleeve. Sew A to A and B to B. Sew left sleeve same as right sleeve (see diagram D on page 58). Sew rem 20 sts on upper sleeves to armhole openings on front and back. Turn sweater RS out.

yoke

All sizes – worked in both lps.

Rnd 1: With RS facing, join yarn with sl st in edge of any row on back neck edge of sweater. Ch 1, sc in same st as joining, sc in valley (between ridges), * sc in top of next ridge, sc in valley, rep from * around. Sl st to first sc. Do not turn.

Rnds 2 and 3: Ch 2 (does not count as a st), hdc in same st as joining, and in each sc around, sl st to first hdc.

Rnds 4 and 5: Ch 2; * hdc in next 9 hdc, sk next hdc: rep from * around; hdc in rem hdc as needed; join with sl st in first hdc.

Rnd 6: (Rnd where ribbon will be placed) Ch 4, tr in next hdc and in each hdc around; join with sl st in 4th ch of beg ch-4.

Rnd 7: Ch 1, sc in same ch as joining, sc in each tr around; join with sl st in first sc.

Rnd 8: Ch 1, sc in same sc as joining and in next 8 sc; * sk next sc, sc in next 9 sc; rep from * around, sc in rem sc as needed; join with sl st in first sc. End off.

optional sleeve cuff

Many sleeves begin at the wrist and can't be lengthened if they're too short, but with this method you can add the optional cuff if you have longer arms.

Rnd 1: With RS of sleeve facing, join yarn with sl st in edge of any row at lower edge of sleeve, ch 1, sc in same st as joining, sc in edge of each row around; join with sl st in first sc.

Rnds 2–7: Ch 2 (does not count as a st), hdc in same stitch as joining and in each st around; join with sl st in first hdc. End off after last row.

Rep rnds 1–7 on other sleeve.

finishing

Weave in loose ends, using a fabric glue such as Aleene's OK To Wash-It to secure ends, if needed. Cut ends of ribbon at a slant and weave through tr rnd of yoke as follows: With front of sweater facing and beg where desired, weave ribbon and tie it into a bow.

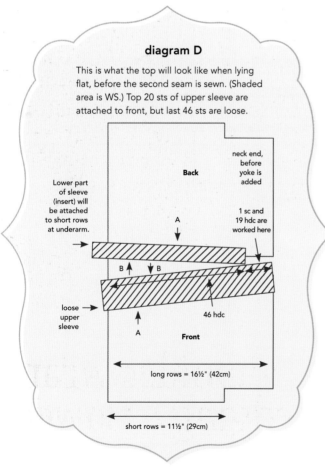

diagram D

This is what the top will look like when lying flat, before the second seam is sewn. (Shaded area is WS.) Top 20 sts of upper sleeve are attached to front, but last 46 sts are loose.

Back

neck end, before yoke is added

Lower part of sleeve (insert) will be attached to short rows at underarm.

1 sc and 19 hdc are worked here

A

B | B

loose upper sleeve

A

46 hdc

Front

long rows = 16½" (42cm)

short rows = 11½" (29cm)

MEDIUM
4
MOYEN
Medio

FINE
2
FIN
Fino

BULKY
5
BULKY
Abultado

The beginner will have no problem making the basic wrap. Dress it up with decorative lace edging and a connective flower, or leave off these adornments for a simpler look.

shoulder wrap
with edging *&* flower

size

Fits sizes XSM–SM (MED–LG, XLG–1X, 2X–3X)

Approx 8" tall x 37" (40", 43", 47") wide; 20cm x 94 (102, 109, 119) cm

materials

Main body: 2 skeins (3 oz/197 yd/85 g per skein) any #4 medium worsted-weight yarn (A)

Used in this project: Lion Brand Wool Ease in Oxford Gray

Edging (optional): approx 1 oz of 1 skein (4 oz/335 yd/113 g) of any #2 fine sport-weight yarn (B)

Used in this project: Red Heart Luster Sheen yarn in black (Substitute: #3 crochet thread)

Flower (optional): approx ½ oz of 1 skein (2.80 oz/84 yd/80 g) of any #5 bulky yarn (C)

Used in this project: Patons Rumor in Hibiscus Heather (Substitute: any #4 medium worsted-weight yarn)

Sizes J/10 (6mm) and G/6 (4mm) crochet hooks for wrap; D/3 (3.25mm) hook for edging; I/9 (5.5mm) for flower

Yarn needle

gauge

With G hook, 6 sl sts = 1" (3cm)

With J hook, 10 dc and 6 dc rows = 3" (8cm)

With D hook, 1 shell = 1¼" (3cm)

With I hook, flower = 3" (8cm) diameter

stitches used

ch, sl st, sc, dc

To work shell: [(dc, ch 2) 4 times, dc] in designated sc.

To work small shell: [(dc, ch 2) 3 times, dc] in designated st.

pattern notes

This wrap is made in one piece with no seam. It has dc worked on the same row with sl sts, which form the ties. Dc stitches (center) are worked in the blo, but the sl sts on the ends (ties) are worked in the flo. This wrap can be made wider or narrower by adding chs to or deleting them from center of beg ch in multiples of 4 and adding same number of dc to each row.

instructions

With color A and G hook, ch 27. Change to J hook and ch 93 (105, 117, 129). Change to G hook and ch 28 – 148 (160, 172, 184) chs.

Row 1: (WS) Loosely sl st in 2nd ch from hook and in next 26 chs. Change to J hook and dc in next 93 (105, 117, 129) chs. Change to G hook and loosely sl st in next 27 chs; turn – 54 sl sts and 93 (105, 117, 129) dc.

Row 2: With G hook, ch 1, sl st loosely in (flo) of next 27 sl sts. Change to J hook and dc in (blo) of next 93 (105, 117, 129) dc. Change to G hook and sl st loosely in (flo) of next 27 sl sts; turn – 54 sl sts and 93 (105, 117, 129) dc.

Rows 3–16: Rep Row 2, 14 times more. End off after last row.

Note: For taller wrap, work more rows.

optional open-shell edging

Sts are worked in both lps.

Row 1: With WS facing and D hook, join color B with sl st in first dc at top edge of wrap, ch 1, sc in same dc as joining; * ch 6, sk next 3 dc, sc in next dc; rep from * across, ending with sc in last dc, sl st in next 2 sl sts on tie; turn.

Row 2: Shell (see Stitches Used on page 60) in first sc; * sc in next ch-6 lp, shell in next sc, rep from * across; sk next sl st on tie, sl st in next sl st, end off – 24 (27, 30, 33) shells. Rep rows 1–2 on opposite edge of wrap.

flower

Sts are worked in both lps.

With I hook and color C, loosely ch 52. Sc in 2nd ch from hook; * sk next ch, small shell (see Stitches Used on page 60) in next ch, sk next ch, sc in next ch; rep from * across to last 6 chs; sl st in last 6 chs. End off, leaving a 14" (36cm) tail – 11 petals (small shells).

Optional: Before rolling petals to form flower, work a sc edging along top edge with color B.

With yarn needle, weave a strand of C through bottom straight edge and pull tail to slightly gather bottom of flower, rolling it with first shell in center and 6 sl sts at outer edge, shaping petals into a rose. Take several sts through all thicknesses to secure in place. To form a circle (in back of flower) stitch tail at end of 6 chs and sl sts to bottom of flower for closure. It will resemble a napkin holder. Weave in ends. Insert ties (sl st ends of wrap) into circle.

SKILL LEVEL:

BULKY
5
BULKY
Abultado

1 **BEGINNER**

2 ADVANCED
BEGINNER

3 INTERMEDIATE

If this sizable bag still isn't big enough to stash all your stuff, make it larger by adding more rows. A tip to remember when making any purse: Crochet tightly so it will be firm enough to hold its contents.

sweater bag

size

Approx 11" (28cm) tall x 18" (46cm) wide (at widest point), 8" (20cm) wide (at top), without handle

materials

3 skeins (3.5 oz/121 yd/100 g per skein) any #5 bulky yarn

Used in this project: Patons Shetland Chunky 75% acrylic/25% wool yarn in Taupe (Substitute: Bernat Softee Chunky, Moda Dea Tweedle Dee or Patons Rumor)

Sizes J/10 (6mm) and G/6 (4mm) crochet hooks

1 brown purse handle with metal rings at ends, any size; handle shown is approx 13" (33cm) when folded

Yarn needle

gauge

With G hook, 10 sc and 9 sc rows = 2" (5cm)

With J hook, 10 dc and 6 dc rows (at widest point) = 3" (8cm)

stitches used

ch, sc, dc

pattern notes

This purse is worked in one piece, folded and seamed up on each side. The narrow top edge is folded over, and then the handle is attached.

instructions

All sts are worked in the blo.

With G hook, ch 22; change to J hook and ch 60; change to G hook and ch 23 – 105 chs.

Row 1: (RS) With G hook, sc in 2nd ch from hook, and in next 21 chs; change to J hook and dc in next 60 chs; change to G hook and sc in rem 22 chs; turn – 104 sts (22 sc, 60 dc, 22 sc) on same row.

Row 2: With G hook, ch 1, sc in blo of first 22 sc; change to J hook and dc in blo of next 60 dc; change to G hook and sc in blo of next 22 sc; turn – 104 sts.

Rows 3–37: Rep Row 2, 35 times more, or for desired width of bag/purse. End off after last row. Fold piece in half with sc sections at top and WS tog. Match up sts on each side and pin in place. Sew side seams and weave in ends.

Note: For a wider or more open neck on the purse, work the sc on each end with a hook larger than size G. Change back to size J hook for dc in center of rows.

Fold top edge over to RS and tack down. Attach handles to inside-top side seams.

getting a handle on it

If you have trouble finding purse handles you like, recycle handles from an old purse you already have or visit a thrift store, where you'll find a variety of purses for a very reasonable price which you can remove the handles from.

SKILL LEVEL:

LIGHT
3
LEGER
Ligero

1 BEGINNER

2 ADVANCED
BEGINNER

3 INTERMEDIATE

If the task of weaving in ends seems like a huge chore, substitute the stripes in this project for a solid color. Try making the top without the turtleneck for a totally different look.

striped, sleeveless turtleneck sweater

size

Fits sizes XSM–SM (MED–LG, XLG–1X, 2X–3X); size shown is a small

Note: See Sizing Information on page 18 to choose appropriate size.

Finished length (all sizes): 23" (58cm) from top of turtleneck to bottom

Finished bust: 31" (38¼", 43½", 50¾"); 79 (97, 110, 129) cm

materials

10 (10, 10, 12) balls (50 g/92 yd per ball) any #3 light worsted-weight yarn: 2 (2, 2, 3) balls in each color

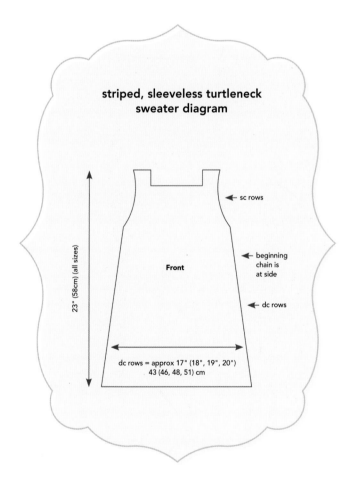

striped, sleeveless turtleneck sweater diagram

23" (58cm) (all sizes)

Front

← sc rows

← beginning chain is at side

← dc rows

dc rows = approx 17" (18", 19", 20")
43 (46, 48, 51) cm

Used in this project: Goshen by Valley Yarns (cotton, modal and silk blend) in Linen (A), Lake (B), Mulberry (C), Purple Haze (D) and Green Apple (E) (Substitute: Caron Simply Soft)

Size G/6 (4mm) crochet hook

Yarn needle

Stitch markers

gauge

14 sc and 11 sc rows = 3" (8cm)

16 dc and 9 dc rows = 4" (10cm)

stitches used

ch, sl st, sc, hdc, dc

pattern notes

Beginning chain is at side seam, and rows are worked vertically. Side and shoulder seams are sewn, and then the turtleneck is worked onto the neck edge and attached as you go.

Color sequence for front and back: A, B, C, D, E

Color sequence for collar: A, C, E, B, D (or desired color sequence)

For a longer top: 4 dc = 1" (3cm), so add 4 more chs per each additional inch desired. Add same number of dc on each row as number of chs added.

For a little girl's dress: Follow the same basic pattern, but use a smaller-weight yarn such as a #2 fine sport-weight. Make your beg ch length needed for any size girl, and then work number of rows needed to fit front of body. Work back same as front.

instructions

All sts are worked in the blo.

front

Notes: Following color sequence (A–E), working 1 row of each color throughout. Rows 1–5 (7, 9, 11) form first shoulder strap at neck edge, and rows 31–35 (37–43, 41–49, 47–57) form 2nd shoulder strap at neck edge.

With A, ch 89. For a longer top, add to the beg ch (see note on page 65).

Row 1: (RS) Sc in 2nd ch from hook, sc in next 27 chs, hdc in next ch, dc in next 59 chs. End off; turn – 88 sts (28 sc, 1 hdc and 59 dc).

Row 2: With WS facing, join B with sl st in blo of first dc, ch 3 (counts as dc), sk first dc, dc in blo of next 58 dc, hdc in blo of next hdc, sc in blo of next 28 sc. End off; turn – 88 sts.

Row 3: With RS facing, join C with sl st in blo of first sc, ch 1, sc in blo of same sc as joining, sc in blo of next 27 sc, hdc in blo of next hdc, dc in blo of next 59 dc. End off; turn – 88 sts.

Rows 4–5 (7, 9, 11): Rep rows 2 and 3, 1 (2, 3, 4) times more, changing color at beg of each row and following color sequence (A–E).

Row 6 (8, 10, 12): With WS facing, join next color yarn with sl st in blo of first dc, ch 3 (counts as dc), sk first dc, dc in blo of next 58 dc, hdc in blo of next hdc, sc in blo of next 19 sc, leaving rem 9 sc unworked (neck edge). End off; turn – 79 sts (59 dc, 1 hdc and 19 sc).

Row 7 (9, 11, 13): With RS facing, join next color

yarn with sl st in blo of first sc, ch 1, sc in blo of same sc as joining, sc in blo of next 18 sc, hdc in blo of next hdc, dc in blo of next 59 dc. End off; turn – 79 sts.

Row 8 (10, 12, 14): With WS facing, join next color yarn with sl st in blo of first dc, ch 3 (counts as dc), sk first dc, dc in blo of next 58 dc, hdc in blo of next hdc, sc in blo of next 19 sc. End off – 79 sts.

Rows 8–30 (10–36, 12–40, 14–46): Rep rows 7–8 (9–10, 11–12, 13–14) appropriate number of times, then rep Row 7 (9, 11, 13) once more, changing color at beg of each row and following color sequence. Hold piece up to body. Keeping in mind that 5 (7, 9, 11) more rows will be worked and piece will stretch because of sts being worked in blo, add or remove rows (in increments of 2 rows) as needed to fit your body.

Row 31 (37, 41, 47): (Rows for other strap) With RS facing, join next color yarn with sl st in blo of first sc, ch 10, sc in 2nd ch from hook and in next 8 chs (9 sc on strap), sc in blo of same sc as joining, sc in blo of next 18 sc, hdc in blo of next hdc, dc in blo of next 59 dc. End off – 88 sts.

Rows 32–35 (38–43, 42–49, 48–57): Rep rows 2 and 3, 2 (3, 4, 5) times more, changing color at beg of each row and following color sequence.

back

Work in same color sequence as front.

With A, ch 80. For a longer top, add same number of beg chs as on front.

Row 1: (WS) sc in 2nd ch from hook and in next 18 chs, hdc in next ch, dc in next 59 chs. End off; turn – 79 sts (19 sc, 1 hdc and 59 dc).

Row 2: With RS facing, join B with sl st in blo of first dc, ch 3 (counts as dc), sk first dc, dc in blo of next 58 dc, hdc in blo of next hdc, sc in blo of next 19 sc. End off – 79 sts.

Row 3: With WS facing, join C with sl st in blo of first sc, ch 1, sc in blo of same sc as joining, sc in blo of next 18 sc, hdc blo of next hdc, dc in blo of next 59 dc. End off; turn – 79 sts.

Rows 4–35 (43, 49, 57): Rep rows 2 and 3 appropriate number of times, changing color at beg of each row and following color sequence (A–E).

side and shoulder seams

With RS tog, match up sts at side of front and back (first and last rows). Place safety pins along edges to hold in place. Beg at bottom st, sew seam up to st number 48 (or to 12th dc below hdc if top is longer) with matching yarn and yarn needle, but do not secure or end off. Rep on other side. With RS tog, match up 5 (7, 9, 11) rows at shoulder strap, and sew

back shoulder seam with yarn and yarn needle. Turn top RS out and try it on to make sure the armholes fit. Adjust by sewing up more or less sts at sides. End off and secure.

turtleneck collar

With RS facing, starting at back, join desired color (or first color of color sequence in Pattern Notes) with sl st in top edge of any sc row. Ch 24.

Note: Colors on collar will not be matched up with colors on front and back, because you will work 1 dc at the end of every 2 sc rows. In other words, you will be skipping every other sc row as you attach collar to neck edge.

Row 1: Dc in 4th ch from hook (3 skipped chs count as dc), dc in each rem ch across. Sk next sc row on neck edge, sl st in edge of next sc row. End off; turn – 22 dc.

Row 2: With WS facing, sk next sc row on neck edge and join next color with sl st in edge of next sc row, dc in blo of each dc across, working last dc in first skipped ch on Row 1. End off; turn – 22 dc.

Row 3: With RS facing, join next color in blo of first dc, ch 3 (counts as dc), sk first dc, dc in blo of next 21 dc, sk next sc row on neck edge, sl st in edge of next sc row. End off – 22 dc.

Row 4: Work same as Row 2, working last dc in 3rd ch of beg ch-3.

Rep rows 3 and 4 around entire neck edge, following color sequence. With RS of Row 1 and last row of collar tog, sew seam, making sure seam is on underside of collar when folded over on outside. Weave in ends.

If desired, tack down folded collar to neck edge on back.

BULKY
5
BULKY
Abultado

1 BEGINNER

2 ADVANCED
BEGINNER

3 INTERMEDIATE

Crochet yourself a pair of these comfy slippers to keep your toes toasty on chilly nights. Elastic woven through the top edge holds them snugly around the foot.

slippers *with* rose

size

Fits women's sizes 5–6 (7–8, 9–10)

Approx 8¾" (10½", 12"); 22 (27, 31) cm long

To custom fit to any size foot, including smaller or larger sizes, see Pattern Notes.

materials

1 skein (3.5 oz per skein) any #5 bulky-weight yarn (A)

Used in this project: Yarn Bee Dreamy Chenille in Dark Plum (Substitutes: Lion Brand Suede or any #4 medium-weight yarn)

1 ball #3 crochet cotton in lavender (for rose) (B)

3 yds #3 crochet thread in green (for leaf) (C)

Sizes J/10 (6mm) and E/4 (3.5mm) crochet hooks

Two black 25" (64cm) strands Dritz Beading Elastic

Yarn needle

gauge

With J hook, 7 sc and 5 sc rows = 2" (5cm)

With E hook, rose = 2½" (6cm) diameter

stitches used

ch, sl st, sc, hdc, dc

pattern notes

The slippers are basically worked in a square in the blo. Ends are seamed, and elastic is woven through top edge to help keep the slippers on the foot. The rose is worked in one long strip and then rolled up.

For smaller foot: Work only enough chs at beg to fit around the sides and bottom of foot. Work less rows, following the pattern, to fit a smaller foot.

For larger foot: Work enough chs at beg to fit around sides and bottom of foot. Following the pattern, work more rows than specified to fit a longer foot.

instructions

All sts are worked in the blo.

Make 2.

For all women's sizes 5–10: with J hook and color A, ch 23. (For wide feet, work more chs here to fit around foot and more sc on each row.)

Row 1: (WS) Sl st in 2nd ch from hook, sc in next 20 chs, sl st in last ch; turn – 22 sts.

Rows 2–22 (26, 30): Ch 1, sl st in blo of first sl st, sc in blo of next 20 sc, sl st in blo of last sl st; turn –

22 sts. End off yarn after last row, leaving a 12" (30cm) tail for sewing seam. Place slipper around foot. Add or delete rows as needed for proper length.

seams

Fold slipper in half widthwise. With RS tog, sew seams at short ends with yarn and yarn needle. Turn RS out. Try slipper on foot to make sure it fits. Add or delete rows to fit, if necessary. With needle, weave elastic through lps on inside of slipper at top edge, pulling elastic so slipper will fit snugly around foot.

Tie ends of elastic to secure. Weave in ends.

rose

Make 2. Worked in both lps.

With E hook and color B, ch 6, leaving a 12" (30cm) tail for gathering bottom edge of flower later.

Row 1: Sc in 2nd ch from hook and in next ch, hdc in next ch, dc in last 2 chs; turn – 5 sts.

Row 2: Ch 3 (counts as dc), sk first dc, dc in next dc, hdc in next hdc, sc in last 2 sc; turn – 5 sts.

Row 3: Ch 1, sc in first 2 sc, hdc in next hdc, dc in next dc, dc in 3rd ch of beg ch-3; turn – 5 sts.

Rows 4–44: Rep rows 2 and 3, 20 times more, ending with a Row 2 rep. Do not end off; turn.

Row 45: Ch 3 (counts as dc), sk first sc, dc in next sc, hdc in next hdc, sc in next dc, sc in 3rd ch of beg ch-3; turn.

Row 46: Rep Row 3.

Rows 47 and 48: Rep rows 2 and 3.

Row 49: Ch 3 (counts as dc), sk first dc, dc in next dc, hdc in next hdc, sl st in last 2 sc. End off. Weave tail at beg of Row 1 through bottom edge of Row 1 over to beg st on Row 1, then through edge of rows and pull to gather, rolling up as you go, with Row 1 in center, so it will form a rose.

leaf

Make 2.

With E hook and color C, ch 12, sl st in 2nd ch from hook, sc in next ch, hdc in next ch, dc in next 8 chs, ch 1, sl st around post of last dc in and in ch at base of last dc, ch 3 (counts as dc), working in free lps of chs on opp side, sk first ch, dc in next 7 chs, hdc in next ch, sc in next ch, sl st in last ch. End off. Weave in ends. Sew leaf and rose to top of slipper as shown in photo.

BULKY
5
BULKY
Abultado

MEDIUM
4
MOYEN
Medio

SKILL LEVEL:

1 BEGINNER

**2 ADVANCED
BEGINNER**

3 INTERMEDIATE

Styled much like the popular fisherman's hat, this hat looks handsome on anyone. This pattern features most of the graduated stitches in the book; however, the bulky tweed yarn makes this a fast one to finish. On page 74 are instructions for making a pair of mittens to match.

flared tweed hat
with mittens

flared tweed hat

size

Fits women's sizes SM, MED and LG

Project model is approx 9" (23cm) from crown to brim x 22" (56cm) circumference.

materials

For body of hat: 1¼ skeins (3 oz/123 yd/85 g per skein) any #5 bulky yarn

Used in this project: Patons Shetland Chunky Tweeds in Earthy Brown

For flower: 1 oz any #4 medium worsted-weight yarn

Used in this project: Moda Dea Washable Wool in Moss Green

Size I/9 (5.5mm) crochet hook

1 flat washable bead, approx ⅝" (2cm) diameter

Matching sewing thread and sewing needle

Yarn needle

gauge

13 dc and 6 dc rows = 4" (10cm)

stitches used

ch, sl st, sc, hdc, dc, htr, tr

pattern notes

This hat is worked from side to side, and all sts are worked in the blo, so the hat will stretch around the head.

instructions

All sts are worked in the blo.

With brown, ch 30.

Row 1: (WS) Working in back bar of chs, sl st in in 2nd ch from hook, sc in next 2 chs, hdc in next ch, dc in next 19 chs, htr in next ch, tr in next 5 chs; turn – 29 sts (including sl st).

Row 2: (RS) Ch 4 (counts as first tr), sk first tr, tr in blo of next 4 tr, htr in blo of next htr, dc in blo of next 19 dc, hdc in blo of next hdc, sc in blo of next 2 sc, sl st in last sl st; turn – 29 sts.

Row 3: Ch 1, sl st in sl st, sc in blo of next 2 sc, hdc in blo of next hdc, dc in blo of next 19 dc, htr in blo of next htr, tr in blo of next 4 tr, tr in 4th ch of beg ch-4; turn – 29 sts.

Rows 4–34: Rep rows 2 and 3, 15 times more, then rep Row 2 once more. End off after last row, leaving an 18" (48cm) tail for sewing side seam.

There is no front and back to this piece. Place foundation ch and last row, with RS tog. Starting at bottom flared edge, sew side seam with tail and yarn needle. With yarn needle, weave yarn through top edges (crown) and pull to gather, closing up hole at top. Secure and end off.

top stitching

With yarn needle and double strand of green, weave yarn through all rows between 8th and 9th sts from the bottom edge (see photo). Secure ends. Weave in all ends.

flower

Sts are worked in both lps.

With green, ch 38.

Sc in 2nd ch from hook; * hdc in next ch, dc in next ch, 3 tr in next ch, dc in next ch, hdc in next ch, sc in next ch; rep from * across – 49 sts (6 petals).

End off, leaving a 10" (25cm) tail. With yarn needle, weave tail through lower straight edge and pull to gather, forming a flower with 6 cupped petals. Sew ends of flower tog to secure.

finishing

Center flower on RS of hat on top of woven strands. Sew flower to side of hat, tying 2–3 knots on WS to secure. Sew bead to center of flower with sewing thread and needle. Weave in ends.

switch it up

Instead of sewing the flower onto the hat, attach a pin in back and use it as a removable accent on a lapel or a purse. Make flowers of many different colors so you can switch them out.

mittens

size

Fits women's sizes XSM–MED (LG–XLG)

Finished length: approx 9" (10"); 23 (25) cm

materials

For body of mittens: 1 skein (3 oz/123 yd/85 g per skein) any #5 bulky yarn

Used in this project: Patons Shetland Chunky Tweeds in Earthy Brown

For flowers: 1 oz any #4 medium worsted-weight yarn

Used in this project: Moda Dea Washable Wool in Moss Green

Sizes I/9 (5.5mm) and J/10 (6mm) crochet hooks (see Pattern Notes)

2 flat washable beads, approx ½" (1cm)

Yarn needle

Stitch markers

gauge

With I hook: 14 dc = 4" (10cm); 7 dc rows = 4" (10cm)

With J hook: 14 dc = 4⅜" (11cm); 7 dc rows = 4 3/8" (11cm)

stitches used

ch, sl st, sc, hdc, dc

pattern notes

For sizes XSM–MED and flowers, use the I hook; use the J hook for sizes LG–XLG. The mittens are worked from side to side, and all sts are worked in the blo. The graduated stitches shape the mittens and form the tightness at the wrists. The cuff is flared and has a green flower attached at the wrist. The mittens have only one seam.

instructions

All sts are worked in the blo.

With appropriate size hook and brown, ch 33.

Row 1: (RS) Working in back bar of chs, sl st in 2nd ch from hook, sc in next ch, dc in next 20 chs, sc in next 4 chs, hdc in next ch, dc in next 5 chs, turn – 32 sts (1 sl st, 1 sc, 20 dc, 4 sc, 1 hdc and 5 dc).

Row 2: Ch 3 (counts as first dc), dc in blo of next 4 dc, hdc in blo of next hdc, sc in blo of next 4 sc, dc in blo of next 20 dc, sc in blo of next sc, sl st in next sl st; turn – 32 sts.

Row 3: Ch 1, sl st in next sl st, sc in blo of next sc, dc in blo of next 20 dc, sc in blo of next 4 sc, hdc in blo of next hdc, dc in blo of next 5 dc; turn – 32 sts.

Rows 4–15: Rep rows 2 and 3, 6 times more. End off after last row.

side seam

With RS tog, fold mitten in half, matching up foundation chs with sts on last row. Place marker through both thicknesses (front and back) in 16th st from end with 5 dc (wrist end). Starting at wrist end, sew a side seam from lower edge up to and including 16th st, with long piece of yarn and yarn needle, using a whip st. Secure last st. End off. Turn mittens RS out.

thumb

Sts are worked in both lps.

Rnd 1: With RS facing, appropriate size hook and seam at left, join brown with sl st in st to right of seam (17th st), ch 2 (counts as first hdc), dc in seam, pivot mitten to left, hdc in next 4 sts on left side edge of mitten (to left of seam); to connect to other side of mitten, take lp off hook, insert hook in 4th st from right side of seam, put lp back on hook and pull lp through st on right side of mitten (to right of seam); ch 2 (counts as hdc), hdc in next 3 sts on right side edge (to right of seam), working last hdc in same st as joining; join with sl st in 2nd ch of beg ch-2, do not turn – 10 sts.

Rnd 2: Ch 2 (counts as hdc), dc in next dc, hdc in next 4 hdc, hdc in 2nd ch of next ch-2, hdc in last 3 hdc; join with sl st in 2nd chain of beg ch-2 – 10 sts.

Rnd 3: Ch 2 (counts as hdc), dc in next dc, hdc in each rem hdc; join with sl st in 2nd ch of beg ch-2 – 10 sts.

Rnds 4–5: Rep Row 3, 2 times more – 10 sts.

Rnd 6: Sl st in each st around. End off, leaving a 6" (15cm) tail. With yarn needle and tail, weave yarn through sl sts on Rnd 6 to close up hole.

Turn mitten WS out. Beginning at sts above thumb, sew remainder of mitten side seam. Do not end off yarn.

Weave yarn through edge of sts on top edge of mitten, pulling tight to close up hole. Sew 1–2 sts through all thicknesses to secure. End off. Turn RS out.

Rep instructions for other mitten. There is no left or right mitten. Weave in ends.

flower

With I hook and green, follow instructions for flower on page 73. Sew flowers to mittens at wrist, same as hat (make sure to sew flowers on opposite sides of mittens to make one left and one right mitten). Sew beads to center of flowers.

SKILL LEVEL:

BULKY
5
BULKY
Abultado

1 BEGINNER

2 ADVANCED BEGINNER

3 INTERMEDIATE

Graduated stitches are what give this scarf a gradual flare at each end. A bulky yarn is best, but the scarf could be made with just about any weight of yarn. Wear it loose around your neck, wrapped around with the ends hanging, or tied into a bow for an ultrafeminine look.

scarf *with* flared ends

size

approx 1½" (center width) x 60" (4cm x 152cm)

materials

1 skein (1.75 oz/90 yd/50 g per skein)
#5 bulky yarn

Used in this project: Bernat Bling Bling in
Spotlight Sage

Size N/15 (10mm) crochet hook

Yarn needle

gauge

5 sc and 4 sc rows = 2" (5cm)

6 dc and 3 dc rows = 2¾" (7cm)

8 tr and 3 tr rows = 4" (10cm)

instructions

Worked in both lps.

Ch 111.

Row 1: Tr in 5th ch from hook (4 sk chs count as
tr), tr in next 7 chs, htr in next 2 chs, dc in next 5
chs, hdc in next 2 chs, sc in next 72 chs, hdc in next
2 chs, dc in next 5 chs, htr in next 2 chs, tr in next 9
chs; turn — 108 sts.

Row 2: Ch 4 (counts as first tr), sk first tr, tr in next
8 tr, htr in next 2 htr, dc in next 5 dc, hdc in next 2
hdc, sc in next 72 sc, hdc in next 2 hdc, dc in next 5
dc, htr in next 2 htr, tr in next 8 tr, tr in first skipped
ch; turn — 108 sts.

stitches used

ch, sc, hdc, dc, htr, tr

pattern notes

For a shorter scarf: Work less chs at beg.

For a wider scarf: Work more rows.

put a bead on it

This beaded version was made with Lion
Brand Suede yarn, in Waterlilies Print. Visit
www.mjcrochet.com for instructions.

Rows 3 and 4: Rep Row 2 twice, working last tr in
4th ch of turning ch-4. End off after last row. Weave
in ends.

FINE
2
FIN
Fino

1 BEGINNER

2 ADVANCED
BEGINNER

3 INTERMEDIATE

This scarf's flirty ruffles are made by using several different stitches with varying heights on the same row. Tiny sequins in the yarn give it a bit of flash. It can be worn as an ascot or tied at the neck, or just let the ends hang loose.

scarf *with* ruffled ends

size

approx 2½" (center width) x 43" (6cm x 109cm)

materials

1 hank (225 yd/100 g per hank) #2 fine sport-weight yarn

Used in this project: South West Trading Company Yang (silk, bamboo and wool blend with sequins) in Celery Green (Substitute: Tilli Tomas Disco Lights, 100% spun silk with sequins)

Size H/8 (5mm) crochet hook

Yarn needle

gauge

13 sc = 4" (10cm); 9 sc rows = 2" (5cm)

6 sts in brackets = 2" (5cm)

stitches used

ch, sc, hdc, dc, htr, tr, hdtr, dtr

pattern notes

The graduated stitches are worked in the blo at the ends of the scarf. The center of the scarf is made using a single crochet worked in the front loop only, creating a different look than the traditional single crochet.

For a wider scarf: Work more rows.

For a longer scarf: Add to your beg ch, remembering to add same number to sc section (center section of scarf).

try it in teal

This bold and beautiful teal version was made with the Tilli Tomas Disco Lights yarn in Jade.

instructions

Ch 143.

Row 1: Working in back bar of chs, hdtr in 6th ch from hook (5 skipped chs count as dtr), tr in next ch, htr in next ch, dc in next ch, hdc in next ch, sc in next 127 chs, hdc in next ch, dc in next ch, htr in next ch, tr in next ch, hdtr in next ch, dtr in last ch; turn – 139 sts.

Row 2: Ch 5 (counts as first dtr), sk first dtr, hdtr in blo of next hdtr, tr in blo of next tr, htr in blo of next htr, dc in blo of next dc, hdc in blo of next hdc, sc in flo of next 127 sc, hdc in blo of next hdc, dc in blo of next dc, htr in blo of next htr, tr in blo of next tr, hdtr in blo of next hdtr, dtr in blo of next dtr; turn – 139 sts.

Rows 3–12: Rep Row 2, 10 times more. End off after last row. Weave in loose ends.

SKILL LEVEL:

BULKY
5
BULKY
Abultado

1 BEGINNER

2 **ADVANCED BEGINNER**

3 INTERMEDIATE

This unique scarf resembles ones that have motifs sewn together, but in this case alternating taller and shorter stitches worked on the same row create the effect. Fringe added with pretty ladder yarn (sometimes called carrying yarn or thread) makes the scarf far from ordinary.

wavy fringed scarf

size

approx 4" x 46" (10cm x 117cm) plus fringe

materials

1 skein (100 g/3.5 oz/164 yd per skein) #5 bulky suedelike yarn (A)

1 ball ladder yarn (B) (sometimes called *carrying* yarn or thread; 12 yds used)

Used in this project: Yarn Bee Dreamy Chenille in Dusty Lilac (Substitute: Lion Brand Suede)

Size N/15 (10mm) crochet hook

Yarn needle

gauge

Each motif of 11 sts = 4" wide x 5¼" long (10cm x 13cm)

stitches used

ch, sc, hdc, dc, tr

Pattern stitch: 2 sc, 1 hdc, 2 dc, 3 tr, 2 dc, 1 hdc (11 sts)

pattern notes

Try not to work sts too tight so scarf won't cup in.

instructions

All sts are worked in both lps.

With 1 strand A and 1 strand B held tog, ch 98.

Row 1: Dc in 3rd ch from hook (2 skipped chs count as hdc), dc in next ch, tr in next 3 chs, dc in next 2 chs, hdc in next ch, (sc in next 2 chs, hdc in next ch, dc in next 2 chs, tr in next 3 chs, dc in next 2 chs, hdc in next ch) 8 times; turn – 97 sts.

Rows 2–4: Ch 2 (counts as first hdc), sk first st, dc in next 2 sts, tr in next 3 sts, dc in next 2 sts, hdc in next st, (sc in next 2 sts, hdc in next st, dc in next 2 sts, tr in next 3 sts, dc in next 2 sts, hdc in next st) 8 times; turn – 97 sts. End off after last row.

fringe

Cut 30 14" (36cm) strands of B. Take 3 strands at a time and fold in half. Attach each set of 3 folded strands to sts at both ends of scarf. Trim ends.

finishing

Weave in ends. You may have to steam this scarf to make it lie flat.

LIGHT
3
LEGER
Ligero

1 BEGINNER

2 ADVANCED
BEGINNER

3 INTERMEDIATE

The beautiful colors of the sock yarn in this head-band—which makes a good ear warmer, too—are perfect for your fall/winter wardrobe. The adjacent single-crochet and triple-crochet stitches create the raised texture.

textured headband 1

size

2¼" x 42" (6cm x 107cm)

One size fits most.

materials

1 skein (50 g/1.76 oz/164 yd per skein)
#3 light worsted-weight yarn

Used in this project: Moda Dea Sassy Stripes
sock yarn in #6250 (Crayon)

Size G/6 (4mm) crochet hook

Yarn needle

gauge

5 sc and 7 sc rows = approx 1¼" (3cm)

8 dc and 6 dc rows in patt = 2" (5cm)

instructions

Ch 174.

Row 1: (RS) Sc in 2nd ch from hook and in
next 43 chs, dc in next 85 chs, sc in last 44
chs; turn – 173 sts.

Row 2: Ch 1, sc in first 44 sc, (sc in next dc, tr in
next dc) 42 times, sc in next dc, sc in last 44 sc;
turn – 173 sts (42 raised sts).

Row 3: Ch 1, sc in first 44 sc, dc in next 85 sts, sc in
last 44 sc; turn – 173 sts.

Rows 4–7: Rep rows 2 and 3 twice. End off after
last row. Weave in loose ends.

stitches used

ch, sc, dc, tr

pattern notes

All sts are worked in both lps. Working a sc next
to a tr is what creates the raised stitches.

For a smoother look: Eliminate the tr and work
all dc in the center section.

For a wider headband: Work more rows.

LIGHT
3
LEGER
Ligero

1 BEGINNER

2 ADVANCED BEGINNER

3 INTERMEDIATE

This headband, made with a cotton-blend yarn that's nice and light for summer, will be less stretchy. With a bulkier, soft yarn and a much larger hook (such as size J, K or N), you can make a scarf instead of a headband (the same goes for the project on page 82).

textured headband 2

size

2½" x 31" (6cm x 79cm)

One size fits most.

materials

1 hank (2 oz/105 yd per hank) #3 light
worsted-weight yarn

Used in this project: Pearls by Prism hand-dyed
yarn in Moss/Olive with metallic threads

Size G/6 (4mm) crochet hook

Yarn needle

gauge

5 sl sts and 8 sl st rows = 1" (3cm)

8 sc and 9 sc/tr rows= 2" (5cm)

instructions

Ch 145.

Row 1: (RS) Sl st in 2nd ch from hook and in next 42
chs, sc in next 58 chs, sl st in last 43 chs; turn – 144
sts (86 sl sts and 58 sc).

Row 2: Ch 1, sl st in first 43 sl sts, sc in next sc, (tr
in next sc, sc in next 2 sc) 19 times, sl st in last 43 sl
sts; turn – 144 sts (19 raised sts).

Row 3: Ch 1, sl st in first 43 sl sts, sc in next 58 sts, sl
st in last 43 sl sts, turn – 144 sts.

Row 4: (Raised sts are staggered on this row.) Ch 1,
sl st in first 43 sl sts (tr in next sc, sc in next 2 sc)

stitches used

ch, sl st, sc, tr

pattern notes

Worked in both lps. Sc next to tr creates the
raised stitches.

19 times, tr in next sc, sl st in last 43 sl sts; turn – 144
sts (20 raised sts).

Row 5: Rep Row 3.

Rows 6–8: Rep rows 2–4.

Row 9: Rep Row 3.

Row 10: Rep Row 2.

Row 11: Rep Row 3. End off. Weave in ends.

LIGHT
3
LEGER
Ligero

1 BEGINNER
2 ADVANCED
   BEGINNER
3 INTERMEDIATE

If smooth is more your style, try making this pretty headband sans the raised stitches.

smooth headband

size

2¼" x 36" (6cm x 91cm)

One size fits most.

materials

1 ball (1.75 oz/200 yd/50 g per ball) variegated #3 lightweight yarn

Used in this project: Bernat Cool Crochet in Tie Dye Shades

Size G/6 (4mm) crochet hook

Yarn needle

gauge

5 sc and 7 sc rows = 1" (3cm)

9 dc and 7 dc rows = 2¼" (6cm)

stitches used

ch, sc, dc

pattern notes

All sts are worked in both lps.

For a wider headband: Work more rows.

instructions

Ch 161.

Row 1: (RS) Sc in 2nd ch from hook and in next 38 chs, dc in next 82 chs, sc in last 39 chs; turn – 160 sts.

Rows 2–7: Ch 1, sc in first 39 sc, dc in next 82 dc, sc in last 39 sc; turn – 160 sts.

End off after last row. Weave in ends.

This simple project can be completed in just thirty minutes. The choker is reversible and can be made longer for a necklace, if you prefer. Make several in different colors for yourself or for your friends.

hemp choker

size

Finished length: 14" (36cm)

One size fits most.

materials

15 yds (14m) fine hemp twine

Used in this project: Darice Fine Hemp Twine in Natural color, available at craft stores (Substitutes: jute or crochet thread)

Size #5 (1.9mm) steel crochet hook

16 tiny wooden beads, with holes large enough for needle to go through, approx 5mm diameter

One ½"–⅝" button (1–2cm)

Yarn needle

Needle (narrow enough to go through holes in beads)

instructions

String beads onto twine with needle.

Ch 98.

Row 1: (WS) Sc in 2nd ch from hook; * hdc in next ch, dc in next ch, 2 tr in next ch, pull up a bead and sl st around it, tr in same ch as 2 tr (you will have 3 tr in 1 ch with a bead in the center st), dc in next ch, hdc in next ch, sc in next ch (shell made); rep from * across. Do not end off – 129 sts (16 shells).

closure loop

Ch 6–10 (depends on the size of your button); turn;

gauge

1 shell = approx ¾" (2cm)

stitches used

ch, sl st, sc, hdc, dc, tr

pattern notes

For a longer choker: Add chs in multiples of 6. Sts are worked in both lps.

sl st in edge of last sc made on Row 1; turn, work 8 – 12 sc in loop; join with sl st in last sl st. End off. Sew button to other end of choker. Weave in ends.

Note: Raised side of choker is shown, but it also can be worn on the opposite side.

SKILL LEVEL:

FINE
2
FIN
Fino

1 **BEGINNER**

2 ADVANCED
BEGINNER

3 INTERMEDIATE

This unique belt is a prime example of how graduated stitching can transform ordinary stitches into an interesting project. The raised texture is created by working in the back loops of each row.

textured belt

size

1½" (4cm) wide x desired length

materials

1 spool (7 oz/200 g per spool) #2 sport-weight yarn

Used in this project: Hilos 100% nylon cord #18 in Olive Green (Substitute: J&P Coats Crochet Nylon cord or any #2, #3 or #4 weight yarn)

Size F/5 (3.75mm) crochet hook

Sewing thread to match cord or yarn

1 belt buckle with 1½" (4cm) center opening

Yarn needle

Sewing needle

gauge

7 sts (sc, hdc, dc, htr, tr, hdtr and dtr) = 1½" (4cm)

3 stitch pattern rows, measured at 2 dtr ends = 2½" (6cm)

instructions

All sts are worked in the blo, creating the ridges.

Ch 8.

Row 1: Sc in 2nd ch from hook, hdc in next ch, dc in next ch, htr in next ch, tr in next ch, hdtr in next ch, dtr in next ch; turn – 7 sts.

Row 2: Ch 1, sc in blo of next dtr, hdc in blo of next hdtr, dc in blo of next tr, htr in blo of next htr, tr in blo of next dc, hdtr in blo of next hdc, dtr in blo of next sc; turn – 7 sts.

stitches used

ch, sc, hdc, dc, htr, tr, hdtr, dtr

pattern notes

You can work this belt in any length for a child or larger adult just by subtracting or adding rows.

Any size yarn or cord can be used, but if you want a wider belt, you'll have to either double the cord/yarn throughout the pattern or use a much bulkier yarn.

For a scarf: Use a bulky yarn and a larger hook with this pattern.

Rep Row 2 for desired length. End off after last row. Weave in ends.

assembly

Loop beg of belt around center post of buckle and sew down end to secure.

SKILL LEVEL:

MEDIUM
4
MOYEN
Medio

1 BEGINNER
2 ADVANCED BEGINNER
3 INTERMEDIATE

Many berets have been spotted on fashion runways lately, but this one is a classic version that will never go out of style.

beret

size

One size fits most.

Project model is approx 12" (30cm) diameter at widest point.

materials

1 skein (3.5 oz/100 g/223 yd per skein) #4 medium worsted-weight yarn

Used in this project: Patons 100% Classic Merino Wool in Deep Olive

Sizes J/10 (6mm) and G/6 (4mm) crochet hooks

Yarn needle

Stitch markers

gauge

With G hook, 4 sc and 4 sc rows (at widest point) = 1" (3cm)

With J hook, 11 hdc and 6 hdc rows = 3" (8cm)

stitches used

ch, sl st, sc, hdc

pattern notes

All sts are worked in the blo. This is a basic rectangle with smaller sts on each end that will shape the hat. The beg ch is at the side seam. After the seam is sewn, the hat becomes a tube, and the crown is made by gathering one edge to form a circle.

For a child's-sized hat: Make your beg ch shorter and work less rows.

instructions

With G hook, ch 1; change to J hook and ch 29; change to G hook and ch 8 – 38 chs.

Row 1: With G hook, sc in 2nd ch from hook and in next 6 chs, pm in last sc made; change to J hook and hdc in next 29 chs; change to G hook and sl st in last ch; turn – 37 sts (7 sc, 29 hdc and 1 sl st).

Row 2: With G hook, ch 1, sl st in blo of first sl st; change to J hook and hdc in blo of next 29 hdc. Take marker out of sc and place in last hdc made; change to G hook and sc in blo of next 7 sc; turn – 37 sts.

Row 3: With G hook, ch 1, sc in blo of first 7 sc. Take marker out of hdc and place in last sc made; change to J hook and hdc in blo of next 29 hdc; change to G hook and sl st in blo of last sl st; turn – 37 sts.

Rows 4–64 (or to desired length): Rep rows 2 and 3 for desired length, ending by working a Row 2 rep. End off after last row, leaving a 20" (51cm) tail for sewing. Match up foundation ch and last row. Pin in place. Sew side seam with tail and yarn needle.

crown

With yarn needle and a 20" (51cm) strand of doubled yarn, weave yarn through sts at ridged sc end of hat. Pull yarn and gather crown into a circle, taking additional sts to close up hole.

Secure and weave in all ends.

Note: If your beret is too big, delete rows. If it's too small, add rows.

CHAPTER THREE

LACY, OPEN~WEAVE GARMENTS

S pace out with these airy projects. The pattern for a stylish baby-doll top can easily be modified to create a dress or skirt. More delicate designs include a soft ruffled shrug and a lovely lacy tunic.

This cute empire-waist top can be worn over a tank top. Leave the straps plain or add a small ruffle at the shoulder. You can make a cute summer dress just by making a longer beginning chain. Later in this chapter you'll learn how to use the instructions for the lower part of this top to make a skirt that flatters any size.

baby-doll top

before you begin
TECHNIQUES YOU WILL USE

This rundown of the techniques used will be useful to read *before* you get started.

The lacy part at the bottom uses the graduated-stitch method with a lacy look, gradually flaring at the bottom.

The bodice is worked in one piece from side to side, with the back-loop-only method, so the bodice will stretch to fit around the bust. It has one seam that will be in the back, forming a tube.

Normally a bodice for this type of top may be worked and gathered at the bottom to fit around the top edge of the lower part of the lacy top. The two pieces would then be sewn together. Sometimes the top edge of a garment is loose, and decreases would have to be made to make it fit around the neck and shoulder area. My second technique with this top is that the shorter single-crochet stitches will shape the bodice (at top and bottom edge) to fit around the bust *without* decreases. The shape will be made as you crochet the rows by using shorter stitches on each end. This way there should be no gathers at the bottom of the bodice, and the top edge of the bodice should fit without having to decrease.

The straps are crocheted right onto the top.

size

Fits sizes XSM (SM, MED, LG, XLG, 1X, 2X, 3X) Note: See Sizing Information on page 18 to choose appropriate size.

Finished length: 20" (51cm) plus straps

Finished bust: approx 29¾" (33½", 37¾", 41½", 45¾", 49½", 53¾", 57½"); 76 (85, 96, 105, 116, 126, 137, 146) cm

materials

6 (9, 11, 13, 15, 17, 19, 21) balls (150 yd per ball) #3 cotton thread

Used in this project: J&P Coats Royale #3 Fashion Crochet 100% cotton thread in Warm Rose (Substitutes: Bernat Cool Crochet or Patons Grace)

Size F/5 (3.75mm) crochet hook

1½–2 yds (137–183cm) of ⅜" (1cm) wide ribbon

Yarn needle

Stitch markers

gauge

Straps: 3 sc = ⅓" (1cm); 16 sc rows = 3" (8cm)

Bodice: 21 dc = 4" (10cm); 11 dc rows = 4" (10cm)

Lower front and back: 1 dc shell = 1" (3cm); 9 dc shell rows = 4" (10cm)

stitches used

ch, sl st, sc, hdc, dc, htr, tr, hdtr, dtr

Special stitches: Dc shell (2 dc, ch 2, 2 dc); htr shell (2 htr, ch 2, 2 htr); tr shell (2 tr, ch 2, 2 tr); hdtr shell (2 hdtr, ch 2, 2 hdtr); dtr shell (2 dtr, ch 2, 2 dtr); to work V-sts (sc, hdc, dc, htr, or tr V-st) (for ruffle on strap), work designated st, ch 2, and designated st in same st [Example: (dc, ch 2, dc) in same st is a dc V-st]

pattern notes

The bodice and skirt of the top are worked in vertical rows from side to side.

For an adult dress: Follow the same instructions for the top, but add to your beginning chain for the extra length. Start with the number of chains called for in the top pattern and add chains in increments of 6. Each 6 chs will add approx 1½" (4cm) to length. Continue with dtr and dtr shells

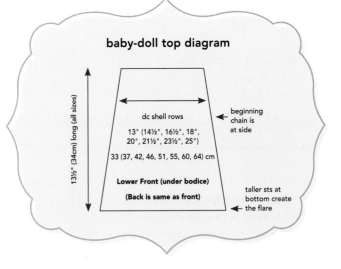

baby-doll top diagram

13½" (34cm) long (all sizes)

dc shell rows

beginning chain is at side

13" (14½", 16½", 18", 20", 21½", 23½", 25")

33 (37, 42, 46, 51, 55, 60, 64) cm

Lower Front (under bodice)

(Back is same as front)

taller sts at bottom create the flare

to the end of your chain, making sure to add the extra dtr and dtr shells on each row as you count. Example: 36 extra chs will add approx 9" (23cm) to length, working 6 more dtr shells and 6 more dtr in each row, following patt as established.

instructions

Beg ch is at side seam, and rows are worked vertically from side to side.

lower front

Worked in both lps.

Ch 62. For longer or shorter top, add or delete chs in increments of 6.

Row 1: (RS) Sc in 2nd ch from hook and in each rem ch across; turn – 61 sc.

Row 2: Ch 3 (counts as dc), sk next 2 sc, dc shell in next sc, [sk next 2 sc, dc in next sc, sk next 2 sc, dc shell in next sc] 2 times; [sk next 2 sc, htr in next sc, sk next 2 sc, htr shell in next sc] 2 times; [sk next 2 sc, tr in next sc, sk next 2 sc, tr shell in next sc] 3 times, sk next 2 sc, hdtr in next sc, sk next 2 sc, hdtr shell in next sc, sk next 2 sc, dtr in next sc, sk next 2 sc, dtr shell in next sc, sk next 2 sc, dtr in last sc; turn – 61 sts (10 shells and 11 sts).

Note: You should have 3 dc shells, 2 htr shells, 3 tr shells, 1 hdtr shell and 1 dtr shell on each row – 10 shells on each row. Piece should measure approximately 13½" (34cm) long.

Row 3: Ch 5 (counts as first dtr), dtr shell in next dtr shell, dtr in next dtr, hdtr shell in next hdtr shell, hdtr in next hdtr, [tr shell in next tr shell, tr in next tr] 3 times, [htr shell in next htr shell, htr in next htr] 2 times, [dc shell in next dc shell, dc in next dc] 2 times, dc shell in last dc shell, dc in 3rd ch of beg ch-3; turn.

Row 4: Ch 3 (counts as dc), dc shell in next dc shell; [dc in next dc, dc shell in next dc shell] 2 times; [htr in next htr, htr shell in next htr shell] 2 times; [tr in next tr, tr shell in next tr shell] 3 times; hdtr in next hdtr, hdtr shell in next hdtr shell; dtr in next dtr, dtr shell in next dtr shell; dtr in 5th ch of beg ch-5; turn.

Rows 5–29 (33, 37, 41, 45, 49, 53, 57): Rep rows 3 and 4 appropriate number of times, ending by working a Row 3 rep. End off after last row. Add more rows if needed.

lower back

Work same as lower front. With RS tog, line up sts at side edges on front and back (first and last rows). Pin in place and sew front to back using yarn and yarn needle, making sure there is a sc row at each side seam. Turn RS out.

At narrow top edge, join thread/yarn with sl st in edge of any st, ch 1, sc in same st as joining, sc evenly spaced around entire top edge, making sure work lies flat; join with sl st in first sc. End off.

bodice

Piece is worked in the blo.

Ch 32. (To shorten or lengthen bodice area that covers bust, add or delete chs here.)

Row 1: Sc in 2nd ch from hook, hdc in next ch, dc in next 27 chs, hdc in next ch, sc in last ch, turn – 31 sts.

Row 2: Ch 1, sc in first sc, hdc in next hdc, dc in next 27 dc, hdc in next hdc, sc in last sc, turn – 31 sts.

Rows 3–82 (92, 104, 114, 126, 136, 148, 158): Rep Row 2 appropriate number of times. Place bodice around bust to make sure it fits. Add or delete rows if needed. End off after last row. With RS tog, match up sts on first and last rows. Sew side seam. Add or delete rows as needed to fit around bust.

bodice attachment to lower piece

With RS tog, place either long edge of bodice tog with narrow top edge of lower front and back, easing in to fit. Secure edges with safety pins, making sure bodice seam is in center back between lower side seams. With thread/yarn and yarn needle, sew bodice to skirt with whip st. Turn top RS out. Join thread/yarn in

st at center top back edge of bodice, ch 1, sc in same st as joining, sc evenly spaced around rem top edge, keeping work flat; join with sl st in first sc. End off.

straps

Worked in both lps.

Try top on and pm where you want straps to be on front and back of top edge of bodice.

Row 1: With RS of front facing, join thread/yarn with sl st in st at right of marker, ch 1, sc in same st as joining, sc in next 2 sts; turn – 3 sc.

Row 2: Ch 1, sc in next 3 sc; turn – 3 sc.

Rows 3–43 (43, 45, 45, 47, 47, 49, 49) or to desired length: Rep Row 2 appropriate number of times.

End off after last row, leaving 6" (15cm) tail. With RS tog, sew end of strap to back of top where marker was placed. End off.

Note: The strap should measure approx 8" (8", 8½", 8½", 9", 9", 9½", 9½"); 20 (20, 22, 22, 23, 23, 24, 24) cm. If you add or delete rows, make sure you work an uneven number so the ruffle will come out right. The strap will stretch, so you may not need more rows.

With RS facing, join thread/yarn with sl st in st on top edge of bodice next to inside neck edge of strap. Sc in edge of each row across neck edge of strap, sl st in next st on bodice edge. End off. Rep on other strap.

optional ruffle for strap

Row 1: With RS facing, join yarn/thread in st on top edge of bodice next to outside edge of strap. Sc in edge of each row across outside edge of strap, sl st in next st on bodice edge. End off.

Row 2: Pm in center st on outside edge of strap (Row 1). Starting from right of center st, count over 21 sts and pm in 21st st. Rep on left side of center st, placing marker at 21st st to left. With RS facing, join thread/yarn with sl st in st to right of marker at far right of strap (on sizes XSM and SM only, this st will be on side edge of bodice at armhole opening). Sl st in st where marker was placed, working along outside edge of strap, sc in next 2 sc, hdc in next 2 sc, dc in next 5 sc, htr in next 3 sc, tr in next 17 sc, htr in next 3 sc, dc in next 5 sc, hdc in next 2 sc, sc in next 2 sc, sl st in st where other marker was placed, sl st in next st on strap (on sizes XSM and SM only, this last sl st will be at side edge of bodice at armhole opening), turn – 45 sts (2 sl sts, 2 sc, 2 hdc, 5 dc, 3 htr, 17 tr, 3 htr, 5 dc, 2 hdc, 2 sc, 2 sl sts).

Row 3: Ch 1, sl st in first 2 sl sts, (sc V-st in next st, sk next st) twice, hdc V-st in next st, (sk next st, dc V-st) 3 times, (sk next st, htr V-st) twice, (sk next st, tr V-st in next st) twice, sk next st, tr shell

in next st (tr shell should be in center st on row), (sk next st, tr V-st in next st) 2 times, (sk next st, htr V-st in next st) 2 times, (sk next st, dc V-st in next st) 3 times, sk next st, hdc V-st in next st, (sk next st, sc V-st in next st) 2 times, sl st in last 2 sts (on sizes XSM and SM only, sl st in next st on side edge of bodice). End off. Rep on other strap.

finishing

With RS facing, work sc evenly spaced around bottom edge of top. End off. Weave in ends. Block top if necessary.

Starting at center front, weave ribbon through sps on each row of lower piece between first dc and dc shell at top edge of lower piece below bodice and tie into a bow.

SKILL LEVEL:

FINE
2
FIN
Fino

1 BEGINNER

2 ADVANCED BEGINNER

3 **INTERMEDIATE**

Your little girl will look adorable in this lacy dress, a pattern based on the baby-doll top on page 96. It's perfect for warmer weather or even for a flower girl to wear in a wedding. The sheen of the specialty yarn gives it sparkle; or make it in an alternate yarn.

little girl's dress

size

Fits sizes 2–3 (4–5, 6–7, 8–10); green dress shown is a size 4–5, and pink dress shown is a size 2–3

Finished length: approx 23¼" (25¾", 28¼", 30¾"); 59 (65, 72, 78) cm long from strap to bottom edging

Chest: approx 21" (23", 25", 27"); 53 (58, 64, 69) cm

materials

For green dress: 3 (3, 4, 5) balls (1.75 oz/ 200 yd/50 g per ball) any #2 fine sport-weight yarn

Used in this project: Bernat Cool Crochet 70% cotton/30% nylon yarn in Sage

For pink dress: 5 (5, 6, 7) balls (1.75 oz/136 yd/ 50 g per ball) any #2 fine sport-weight yarn

Used in this project: Patons Grace 100% cotton in Blush

(Substitute for either dress: J&P Coats Royale #3 Fashion Crochet cotton thread)

Sizes G/6 (4mm) and F/5 (3.75mm) crochet hooks

1½ yds (137cm) of ⅜" (1cm) wide ribbon

2–3 hooks and eyes or snaps for closure in back of dress

Optional: 1 yd (91cm) matching fabric for lining

Yarn needle

gauge

Skirt: With G hook, 1 dc shell and 1 htr = 1¼" (3cm); 2 dc shell rows = 1" (3cm); 1 tr shell and 1 tr = 1½" (4cm); 2 tr shell rows = 1¼" (3cm)

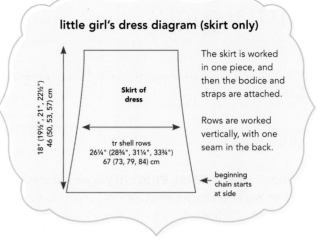

little girl's dress diagram (skirt only)

Skirt of dress

tr shell rows 26¼" (28¾", 31¼", 33¾") 67 (73, 79, 84) cm

18" (19½", 21", 22½") 46 (50, 53, 57) cm

The skirt is worked in one piece, and then the bodice and straps are attached.

Rows are worked vertically, with one seam in the back.

beginning chain starts at side

Bodice: 10 dc and 6 dc rows = 2" (5.1cm)

Straps: 3 sc and 2 sc rows = ½" (1cm)

stitches used

ch, sl st, sc, dc, htr, tr, hdtr, dtr

Special stitches: dc shell (2 dc, ch 2, 2 dc); htr shell (2 htr, ch 2, 2 htr); tr shell (2 tr, ch 2, 2 tr); hdtr shell (2 hdtr, ch 2, 2 hdtr); dtr shell (2 dtr, ch 2, 2 dtr)

pattern notes

This dress is worked similar to the baby-doll top on page 96. The bodice will be worked in both loops (not back loop only like the adult top), because the bust area does not need to stretch. The skirt of this dress is also worked in both loops and will be made in one piece, with only one seam in the back. Custom fit this dress to your child by adding or eliminating vertical rows.

When working shell in shell of previous row, work shell in center ch-2 sp of shell on previous row.

Finishing details: You may need to steam block this dress. The optional lining requires some sewing knowledge. Another option: Wear a slip.

instructions

Beg ch will become seam in the back. Sts are worked in both lps.

skirt front

With G hook, ch 75 (81, 87, 93). (If you want the dress to be longer or shorter, work more or less chs in multiples of 6.) Each set of 6 chs will create 1 more shell and a single st and will make the dress approx 1½" (4cm) longer. Just add more tr shells and tr on each row.

Row 1: (RS) Dc shell in 6th ch from hook (first 3 skipped chs count as dc), sk next 2 chs, htr in next ch, sk next 2 chs, htr shell in next ch, (sk next 2 chs, tr in next ch, sk next 2 chs, tr shell in next ch) 7 (8, 9, 10) times; (sk next 2 chs, hdtr in next ch, sk 2 chs, hdtr shell in next ch) 2 times; sk next 2 chs; dtr in next ch, sk next 2 chs, dtr shell in next ch, sk next 2 chs, dtr in last ch; turn. You should have 1 dc shell, 1 htr shell, 7 (8, 9, 10) tr shells, 2 hdtr shells and 1 dtr shell on row with single sts between each shell. You will also have 1 dc at dc shell end and 1 dtr at dtr shell end – 12 (13, 14, 15) total shells on each row. Row should measure approx 18" (19½", 21", 22½"); 46 (50, 53, 57) cm.

Row 2: Ch 5 (counts as dtr), dtr shell in next dtr shell, dtr in next dtr, (hdtr shell in next hdtr shell, hdtr in next hdtr) 2 times, (tr shell in next tr shell, tr in next tr) 7 (8, 9, 10) times; htr shell in next htr shell, htr in next htr; dc shell in next dc shell, dc in first skipped ch on Row 1; turn – 12 (13, 14, 15) shells.

Row 3: Ch 3 (counts as dc), dc shell in next dc shell; htr in next htr, htr shell in next htr shell; (tr in next tr, tr shell in next tr shell) 7 (8, 9, 10) times; (hdtr in next hdtr, hdtr shell in next hdtr shell) 2 times; dtr in next dtr, dtr shell in next dtr shell, dtr in 5th ch of beg ch-5; turn – 12 (13, 14, 15) shells.

Row 4: Work same as Row 2, working last dc in 3rd ch of beg ch-3.

Rows 5–42 (46, 50, 54): Rep rows 3 and 4 appropriate number of times. End off after last row. Add more or less rows than indicated if the designated number of rows do not fit around the child's body. Work even number of rows if working shell edging.

bodice

Worked in both lps.

Row 1: With RS facing and G hook, join yarn with sl st in top right corner of narrow edge of dress skirt (3rd skipped ch at beg of Row 1), ch 1, sc in same ch as joining, sc in next ch; * 3 sc around dc post on next row ** ; 2 sc in beg ch-3 sp on next row; rep from * across top edge of skirt, ending last rep at ** ; turn – 105 (115, 125, 135) sc.

Row 2: Ch 3 (counts as dc), sk first sc, dc in next sc and in each sc across; turn – 105 (115, 125, 135) dc.

Row 3: Ch 3 (counts as dc), sk first dc, dc in next dc and in each dc across; turn – 105 (115, 125, 135) dc.

Rows 4–8 (10, 12, 14): Rep Row 3, 5 times more. End off after last row. You may want to add or eliminate rows depending on desired length.

back seam of dress

With RS of dress tog, line up sts and pin in place. Beg at lower edge, sew back seam loosely with yarn and yarn needle up to bottom of bodice (this will be up to the first row of bodice). Bodice back will be left open, and snaps or hooks will be sewn there later.

straps

Worked in both lps.

Pm in 11th (15th, 19th, 23rd) st and in 41st (44th, 47th, 50th) st to right and left of back on top edge of bodice.

Row 1: With RS of front facing and G hook, join yarn with sl st in st to right of marker, ch 1, sc in same st, sc in next 2 sts; turn – 3 sc.

Rows 2–21 (25, 29, 33) or to desired length: Ch 1, sc in each sc across; turn – 3 sc.

End off after last row. Try on dress and make sure straps are the right length. If you add rows (in multiples of 4), keep in mind that the strap will stretch. With RS tog, center and sew end of strap to back of top where markers were placed. Rep on other strap. There should be 9 (13, 17, 21) dc from center of back to back of strap and 21 (25, 29, 33) dc between straps on center of front.

shell edging (on top of dress, straps)

With RS facing and F hook, join yarn with sl st in first dc on top back edge of bodice, ch 1, sc in same dc as joining, [sk next dc, 5 dc in next dc (shell made), sk next dc, sc in next dc] 2 (3, 4, 5) times (last sc should be worked in st next to strap); sc in edge of first row on strap, [sk next row, 5 dc in edge of next row (shell made), sk next row, sc in edge of next row] 5 (6, 7, 8) times (last sc should be worked in edge of last row on strap); sc in next dc on top front edge of bodice, [sk next dc, 5 dc in next dc (shell made), sk next dc, sc in next dc] 5 (6, 7, 8) times (last sc should be worked in st next to strap); sc in edge of first row on next strap, [sk next row, 5 dc in edge of next row (shell made), sk next row, sc in edge of next row] 5 (6, 7, 8) times (last sc should be worked in edge of last row on strap); sc in next dc on top back edge of bodice, [sk next dc, 5 dc in next dc (shell made), sk next dc, sc in next dc] 2 (3, 4, 5) times (last sc should be worked in last dc on top back edge of bodice) – 9 (12, 15, 18) shells across top edge of bodice and 5 (6, 7, 8) shells along edge of each strap. End off.

armhole

With RS facing and F hook, join yarn with sl st in st to right of unworked edge of either strap on top edge of bodice, sc in edge of first row on strap, [sk next row, 5 dc in edge of next row (shell made), sk next row, sc in edge of next row] 5 (6, 7, 8) times, sl st in next st on top armhole edge of bodice – 5 (6, 7, 8) shells. End off. Rep on unworked edge of other strap.

optional shell edging (on bottom)

With RS facing and F hook, join yarn with sl st in st at center back seam on bottom edge of dress, ch 1, sc in same st as joining; * 5 dc in center of next dtr or in 3rd ch of next ch-5 sp, sc in st at base of same dtr or in base of same ch-5 sp; rep from * around, ending with sl st in first sc – 42 (46, 50, 54) shells.

Note: If you added more rows to the skirt, you should have the same number of shells as the number of rows you worked on the skirt.

optional lining

Measure lacy skirt of dress to determine length of lining. Add 1"–2" (3–5cm) (for folding over) at top and same amount at bottom of fabric (for hem). For width of lining, double the width of skirt below bodice and add 2"–3" (5–8cm). For example: your lining on the size 2–3 should be at least 20" (51cm) long × 23" (58cm) wide. Cut fabric to proper measurements. Fold bottom edge over ¼" (1cm) and sew in place by machine or hand. Fold top edge over ¼" (1cm) twice and sew in place. Bottom hem will be determined by length and size of dress you are making. Fold lining in half with RS of side edges tog. Starting at top, sew back center seam, leaving about 6" (15cm) open at the bottom (for slit at bottom of lining). Gather top edge of lining with long sts so it will fit around bodice. With RS of lining toward inside of dress, pin gathered top edge of lining to Row 2 of bodice with lining seam and skirt seams matching. With sewing needle and thread, hand st in place.

finishing

Weave in ends. Sew hook and eye or snaps on each side of bodice in back. Starting at center front, weave ribbon through sps between dc and dc shells below bodice at top edge of skirt and tie into a bow.

SKILL LEVEL:

FINE
2
FIN
Fino

1 BEGINNER

2 ADVANCED BEGINNER

3 INTERMEDIATE

This charming skirt is worked the same as the lower part of the baby-doll top on page 96, only longer. The taller stitches at the bottom are what form the pretty flare. Make the skirt shorter or longer to suit your style, or add an optional edging for a dressier look. You might wear it as a strapless dress in the summertime because it stretches to fit around the body.

long flared skirt

size

Fits sizes XSM (SM, MED, LG, XLG, 1X, 2X, 3X)

Finished length: approx 31" (79cm) long, all sizes

Hip approx 31" (33", 35", 37", 39", 41", 43", 45"); 79 (84, 89, 94, 99, 104, 109, 114) cm

See Pattern Notes to custom fit for larger or smaller sizes.

materials

4 (4, 5, 5, 6, 6, 7, 7) skeins (3.52 oz/218 yd per skein) any #2 fine sport-weight yarn

Used in this project: Sinfonia 100% mercerized cotton in Khaki (available at Hobby Lobby, www.crochetstyleetc.com and www.craftsetc.com) (Substitutes: Patons Grace, Patons Brilliant, Bernat Satin Sport)

Size G/6 (4mm) crochet hook

Yarn needle

Stitch markers

gauge

Be sure to check your gauge. If gauge does not match, change to larger or smaller hook.

3 dc shells + 3 dc in patt and 8 dc shell rows = 4" (10cm)

6 chs (1 shell) = approx 1⅜" (3cm)

stitches used

ch, sl st, sc, dc, htr, tr, hdtr, dtr

Special stitches: dc shell (2 dc, ch 2, 2 dc); htr shell (2 htr, ch 2, 2 htr); tr shell (2 tr, ch 2, 2 tr); hdtr shell (2 hdtr, ch 2, 2 hdtr); dtr shell (2 dtr, ch 2, 2 dtr); picot (ch 3, sl st in 3rd ch from hook)

pattern notes

Beg ch and rows are worked vertically, with one seam in back. The drawstring waist is at the hip, and an optional edging is added to the bottom edge.

For a shorter skirt: Work less chs at beg by eliminating 6 chs per shell and working less dc shells on each pattern row.

For a longer skirt: Work more chs at beg in multiples of 6 till you get the desired length, and then add to number of dc shells on each pattern row (15 dc shells + extra shells).

For a custom-fit larger or smaller skirt: (For sizes larger than 3X or smaller than adult XSM) Work beg ch the length you want (in multiples of 6 plus 3 on beg ch, for a toddler or even a size 6X). Following skirt pattern, work as many dc shells as needed, 1 htr shell, 1 tr shell, 1 hdtr shell, and 1 dtr shell at bottom of skirt if you want the flare. Work as many rows as needed to fit around body, and then follow the instructions for drawstring and edging, if desired. To omit flare, omit taller shells and taller sts at bottom of each row and work only dc shells, and dc across entire row.

For a straight skirt minus the flare: Work all dc shells and dc to the end of each row and omit the taller sts at the bottom of skirt.

For a looser fit: If you do not like the "mermaid" look, just add more rows.

For a strapless drawstring dress: Make the dress the same as the skirt and tie the drawstring above the bust. Add more chs in multiples of 6 at beg for a longer dress.

instructions

Work in both lps.

For all sizes: ch 117.

Beg ch should measure approx 32" (81cm) when slightly stretched.

Row 1: (RS) Dc shell in 6th ch from hook (first 3 skipped chs count as dc); (sk next 2 chs, dc in next ch, sk next 2 chs, dc shell in next ch) 14 times; sk next 2 chs, htr in next ch, sk next 2 chs, htr shell in next ch; sk next 2 chs, tr in next ch, sk next 2 chs, tr shell in next ch; sk next 2 chs, hdtr in next ch, sk next 2 chs, hdtr shell in next ch; sk next 2 chs, dtr in next ch, sk next 2 chs, dtr shell in next ch; sk next 2 chs, dtr in last ch; turn – 19 shells with one st between each shell, 1 dc at beg and 1 dtr at end. Row should measure approx 29" (74cm).

Row 2: Ch 5 (counts as first dtr), dtr shell in next dtr shell, dtr in next dtr, hdtr shell in next hdtr shell, hdtr in next hdtr, tr shell in next tr shell, tr in next tr, htr shell in next htr shell, htr in next htr, (dc shell in next dc shell, dc in next dc) 15 times, ending with last dc in first skipped ch at beg of Row 1; turn – 19 shells.

the side-to-side advantage

The incredible thing about this method of crocheting (side to side) is that all you have to do is add more or less rows than indicated if the designated number of rows are not right for you. This goes for all of the garments in this book.

long flared skirt diagram

29" (74cm) without edging (all sizes)

dc shell rows

Hip: 31" (33", 35", 37", 39", 41", 43", 45")
79 (84, 89, 94, 99, 104, 109, 114) cm

beginning chain starts in back, where seam will be

This skirt is worked in one piece and seamed in the back.

Rows are worked vertically.

Row 3: Ch 3 (counts as first dc), dc shell in next dc shell, (dc in next dc, dc shell in next dc shell) 14 times, htr in next htr, htr shell in next htr shell, tr in next tr, tr shell in next tr shell, hdtr in next hdtr, hdtr shell in next hdt shell, dtr in next dtr, dtr shell in next dtr shell, dtr in 5th ch of beg ch-5, turn – 19 shells.

Row 4: Work same as Row 2, ending with last dc in 3rd ch of beg ch-3.

Rows 5–62 (66, 70, 74, 78, 82, 86, 90) or to desired width: Rep rows 3 and 4 appropriate number of times. End off after last row. Number of rows for each larger size listed (mermaid fit) will give a 2" (5cm) increase in size. Add more or less rows in multiples of 2 rows to fit around body. This skirt will stretch, so even if it looks small, it may be a perfect fit. With RS tog, line up sts on foundation ch and last row. Sew back seam with yarn and yarn needle.

waist and drawstring

Note: Waist is meant to be at hip.

Turn skirt RS out. Join yarn with sl st in any sp at waist edge (dc end), ch 5 (counts as first dc and ch-2 sp); * dc in next sp, ch 2; rep from * around entire top edge; sl st in 3rd ch of beg ch-5 – same number of ch-2 sps as number of rows. End off.

Drawstring: Ch 250. End off. Beginning at center front of skirt, weave drawstring through ch-2 sps around top edge and tie into a bow. Adjust ch length if needed. Weave in ends.

optional edging

Rnd 1: With RS facing, join yarn with sl st in top of any dtr on bottom edge of skirt. Working in top ch of beg ch-5 or in top of dtr on each row, ch 7; * sc in top of next row, ch 7; rep from * around; join with sl st in joining sl st – same number of ch-7 sps as number of rows. Do not end off.

Rnd 2: Sl st in next ch-7 sp, ch 3 (counts as first dc); in same ch-7 sp work [picot, dc, picot, htr, (picot, tr) 2 times, picot, htr, (picot, dc) 2 times], sc in next ch-7 sp, * in next ch-7 sp work [(dc, picot) 2 times, htr, (picot, tr) 2 times, picot, htr, (picot, dc) 2 times]; rep from * around; join with sl st in 3rd ch of beg ch-3. End off. Total number of shells will be half the number of rows worked on skirt. Weave in ends.

SUPER FINE
1
SUPER FIN
Super Fino

1 BEGINNER

2 **ADVANCED BEGINNER**

3 INTERMEDIATE

Using a smaller yarn with a larger hook is what makes this light and delicate shrug so soft and drapeable.

ruffled shrug

stitches used

ch, sl st, dc, tr

pattern notes

This shrug is worked in horizontal rows, from one sleeve across back to other sleeve. The long edge is the foundation chain. Ruffles are worked onto the shrug sleeves as you go, which allows you to avoid the task of sewing them on later. All sts are worked in both lps.

size

Fits sizes XSM–SM (MED–LG, XLG–1X, 2X–3X)

Finished measurements before sewing seam: approx 16½" (17¾", 19½", 20½") x 47½" (51½", 55½", 57½"); 42 (45, 50, 52) cm x 121 (131, 141, 146) cm

materials

1 (2, 2, 3) balls (88 oz/249 yd/25 g per ball) any #1 super-fine fingering-weight yarn

Used in this project: Crystal Palace Kid Merino in Roses (Substitute: Knit Picks Palette or Patons Baby yarn)

Size I/9 (5.5mm) crochet hook

Yarn needle

Stitch markers

gauge

8 dc with ch-1 sp between each = 4" (10cm)

7 dc rows = 4" (10cm)

instructions

Ch 172 (186, 200, 206).

Note: If you want sleeves to be longer, work more chs in multiples of 2. Then work more dc and ch-1 sps in center of rows between triple crochets. In other words, if you work 174 chains, that will give you one more dc and ch-1 sp, and you would have 75 dc in center of the row instead of 74.

Row 1: Tr in 8th ch from hook (skipped chs count as tr and ch-1 sp), (ch 1, sk next ch, tr in next ch) 3 times, (ch 1, sk 1 ch, dc in next ch) 74 (81, 88, 91) times. Pm in last dc made. (Ch 1, sk next ch, tr in next ch) 5 times; turn – 84 (91, 98, 101) sts and 83 (90, 97, 100) ch-1 sps. Place Row 1 across arms and back to check length. If necessary, adjust length as desired before proceeding. Adjust number of (dc, ch 1) on each row also.

Row 2: Ch 4 (counts as first tr), (ch 1, sk next ch-1 sp, tr in next tr) 4 times, (ch 1, sk next ch-1 sp, dc in next dc) 74 (81, 88, 91) times, (ch 1, sk next ch-1 sp, tr in next tr) 4 times, ch 1, sk next ch, tr in next ch; turn – 84 (91, 98, 101) sts and 83 (90, 97, 100) ch-1 sps.

Rows 3–29 (31, 34, 36): Rep Row 2 appropriate number of times, ending off after last row.

sleeve seams

Fold shrug in half widthwise (across arms). Match up sts and ch-1 sps on first and last rows. Place markers or pieces of yarn to hold in place. Count over 22 sps and pm at 22nd sp. Starting at ruffled edge (arm opening), attach yarn and sl st loosely to 22nd sp (where marker was placed), sewing arm seam. Option: You can sew the seam with yarn needle and yarn with whip st if you prefer. Rep on other side for other sleeve. Turn shrug RS out. Try shrug on to check armhole depths/sleeve seams and adjust if necessary.

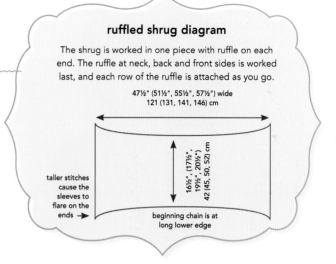

ruffled shrug diagram

The shrug is worked in one piece with ruffle on each end. The ruffle at neck, back and front sides is worked last, and each row of the ruffle is attached as you go.

47½" (51½", 55½", 57½") wide
121 (131, 141, 146) cm

16½", (17½", 19½", 20½")
42 (45, 50, 52) cm

taller stitches cause the sleeves to flare on the ends →

beginning chain is at long lower edge

ruffle

Work around entire neck and bottom edge.

With RS facing, join yarn with sl st in any dc on back neck edge, ch 17.

Row 1: Tr in 8th ch from hook (skipped chs count as tr and ch-1 sp), (ch 1, sk next ch, tr in next ch) 2 times, (ch 1, sk next ch, dc in next ch) 2 times, ch 1, sl st in next (dc, ch-1 sp and dc) on shrug edge; turn – 4 tr, 2 dc and 6 ch-1 sps.

Row 2: (Ch 1, sk next ch-1 sp, dc in next dc) 2 times, (ch 1, sk next ch-1 sp, tr in next tr) 4 times, working last tr in 2nd skipped ch at beg of Row 1; turn – 2 dc, 4 tr and 6 ch-1 sps.

Row 3: Ch 5 (counts as first tr and ch-1 sp), sk first tr, tr in next tr, (ch 1, sk next ch-1 sp, tr in next tr) 2 times, (ch 1, sk next ch-1 sp, dc in next dc) 2 times, ch 1, sl st in next (dc, ch-1 sp and dc) on shrug edge, sl st around next ch-1 sp on edge, sl st to top of next dc on shrug edge, turn – 4 tr, 2 ch and 6 ch-1 sps.

Row 4: Work same as Row 2, working last tr in 4th ch of turning ch-5; turn.

Rep rows 3 and 4 around entire shrug opening edge. End off after last row. With RS tog, sew first and last rows of ruffle tog, matching up sps, same as sleeve seams. Weave in ends.

FINE
2
FIN
Fino

1 BEGINNER

2 ADVANCED
BEGINNER

3 INTERMEDIATE

This tunic's features—
higher neckline, side slits,
looser fit and longer length—
were designed with the fuller
figured woman in mind, but
the garment looks fabulous
on smaller sizes, too. For a
simpler look, try it in a
solid color.

lacy tunic

size

Fits sizes XSM–SM (MED–LG, XLG–1X, 2X–3X); size shown is XLG

Finished bust: approx 33" (40½", 48", 55½"); 84 (103, 122, 141) cm

Finished length: approx 23" (23", 24", 24"); 58 (58, 61, 61) cm, before stretching

materials

1 hank (16 oz/1400 yd hank) any #2 fine sport-weight yarn

Used in this project: Interlacements Rick Rack II 100% rayon yarn in Renaissance (Substitutes: Bernat Cool Crochet, Patons Brilliant)

Size H/8 (5mm) crochet hook

1½–3 yds (137–274cm) of 1" (3cm) wide ribbon (optional)

Yarn needle

Stitch markers

gauge

1 dc cluster = ⅝" (2cm) wide

2 dc clusters, 2 sc and 4 ch-4 sps in patt = 3¾" (10cm)

3 dc cluster rows and 3 ch-4 rows in patt = 3" (8cm)

stitches used

ch, sl st, sc, dc, tr, dtr

To work dc cluster: (Yo, draw up a lp in designated ch-4 sp, yo and draw through 2 lps on hook) 4 times, yo and draw through 4 lps on hook, yo and draw through last 2 lps on hook.

To work tr cluster: * Yo twice, draw up a lp in designated ch-4 sp, (yo and draw through 2 lps on hook) 2 times; rep from * 3 times more; yo and draw through 4 lps on hook, yo and draw through last 2 lps on hook.

To work dtr cluster: * Yo 3 times, draw up a lp in designated ch-4 sp, (yo and draw through 2 lps on hook) 3 times; rep from * 3 times more; yo and draw through 4 lps on hook, yo and draw through last 2 lps on hook.

pattern notes

This tunic is worked in one piece, and then the side and underarm seams are sewn. Flare at the bottom of tunic and on the ends of the sleeves is created by working taller stitches. This tunic is very stretchy, so keep that in mind when choosing size to make. Gauge is crucial; if yours does not match what is listed, change to a different-size hook.

instructions

All sts are worked in both lps.

tunic front (at bottom)

Beg ch is at side seam.

All sizes: Ch 56 to measure approx 14" (36cm) without stretching.

Row 1: Sc in 8th ch from hook (skipped chs count as ch-4 sp); * ch 4, sk next 3 chs, sc in next ch; rep from * to end, turn – 13 ch-4 sps.

Row 2: (Ch 4, dc cluster in next ch-4 sp, ch 4, sc in next ch-4 sp) twice, (ch 5, tr cluster in next ch-4 sp, ch 5, sc in next ch-4 sp) 4 times, ch 5, tr cluster in last ch-4 sp, dtr in 4th skipped ch; turn – 7 clusters total (2 dc clusters and 5 tr clusters).

Row 3: * Ch 4, sc in next ch-4 sp; rep from * across, ending with last sc in turning ch-4 sp; turn – 13 ch-4 sps.

Row 4: Work same as Row 2, ending with dtr in top of dtr on row before last row; turn. Piece should now measure approx 13" (33cm) – 7 clusters.

Rows 5–35 (43, 51, 59): Rep rows 3 and 4 appropriate number of times, ending with a Row 3 rep. End off after last row.

front bodice and sleeves

Front: Pm on side you have indicated as RS. With RS facing, join yarn with sl st in top left-hand corner of piece, (dc cluster edge), ch 52 for right sleeve. End off. With RS facing, join yarn with sl st in top right-hand corner, ch 53 for left sleeve. Do not end off.

Row 1: Sc in 2nd ch from hook; * ch 4, sk next 3 chs, sc in next ch; rep from * across to end of ch 53, working last sc in corner sc of tunic front, ** ch 4, sk next cluster row, sc in next sc between cluster rows; rep from ** across to corner, working last sc in left corner sc of tunic front, *** ch 4, sk next 3 chs, sc in next ch; rep from *** across to end of ch 52, working last sc in last ch; turn – 43 (47, 51, 55) ch-4 sps.

Row 2: Ch 6, dtr cluster in first ch-4 sp, ch 6, sc in next ch-4 sp, ch 5, tr cluster in next ch-4 sp, ch 5, sc in next ch-4 sp, (ch 4, dc cluster in next ch-4 sp, ch 4, sc in next ch-4 sp) 18 (20, 22, 24) times; ch 5, tr cluster in next ch-4 sp, ch 5, sc in next ch-4 sp, ch 6, dtr cluster in last ch-4 sp, dtr in last sc; turn. You should have 22 (24, 26, 28) total clusters on each cluster row. You'll have 1 dtr cluster and 1 tr cluster at each end and 18 (20, 22, 24) dc clusters between the ends. All sizes – 7 clusters on each sleeve.

Row 3: * Ch 4, sc in next ch-sp; rep from * across,
ending with last sc in turning ch-6 sp; turn – 43 (47, 51, 55) ch-4 sps.

Row 4: Work same as Row 2, ending with dtr in top of dtr on row before last row; turn.

Rows 5–16 (16, 18, 18): Rep rows 3 and 4 appropriate number of times.

left shoulder and top of sleeve

Row 1: [Ch 4, sc in next ch-sp] 19 (21, 23, 25) times; turn – 19 (21, 23, 25) ch-4 sps.

Row 2: [Ch 4, dc cluster in next ch-4 sp, ch 4, sc in next ch-4 sp] 8 (9, 10, 11) times; ch 5, tr cluster in next ch-4 sp, ch 5, sc in next ch-4 sp; ch 6, dtr cluster in last ch-4 sp, dtr in top of dtr on row before last row; turn –10 (11, 12, 13) clusters.

Row 3: * Ch 4, sc in next ch-sp; rep from * across, ending with last sc in turning ch-4 sp; turn – 19 (21, 23, 25) ch-4 sps.

Row 4: Rep Row 2.

Row 5: Rep Row 3. End off.

right shoulder and top of sleeve

Row 1 on opposite side. With WS facing, join yarn with sl st in top of first dtr on other sleeve end. Rep rows 1–5 of left shoulder. You will have 10 (11, 12, 13) clusters at top of each sleeve (from neck edge to end of sleeve).

back bodice and sleeves

Row 1: With RS facing, join yarn with sl st in last sc on Row 5 of left shoulder. Loosely ch 19. Without twisting ch, join with sl st in last sc on rows of right shoulder; turn, (ch 4, sk next 3 chs, sc in next ch) 5 times, ending with sl st in joining sl st – 5 ch-4 sps. End off. Try on tunic, and if you decide you want neck opening to be bigger, you'll need to take out this ch 19 and 5 ch-4 sps, add more rows in multiples of 2 to both shoulder areas (which would be added to Row 25 of shoulder), then rework this ch 19 and 5 ch-4 sps.

Row 2: With WS facing, join yarn with sl st in first sc on Row 5 of right shoulder, rep Row 2 of Front Bodice and Sleeves.

Rows 3–16 (16, 18, 18): Rep rows 3–16 (16, 18, 18) of Front Bodice and Sleeves. End off after last row.

tunic back (at bottom)

Lay tunic on flat surface and turn so the last row you worked is at the top. Count over 13 ch-4 sps on last row from end of each sleeve and pm in next sc on each sleeve. There should be 17 (21, 25, 29) ch-4 sps between markers. Turn piece sideways so the front is to your left, one sleeve is at the top and other sleeve is at the bottom. Working edge of rows in space between markers, on back bodice, join yarn with sl st in sc where you placed lower marker (see diagram). Ch 56.

Row 1: Rep Row 1 of tunic front – 13 ch-4 sps. After last sc is worked in last ch, sl st in sc on edge of back bodice (where beg ch was joined). Sl st in next 4 chs of next ch-4 sp on edge on back bodice so you will be at height of dc to work first dc cluster when you turn for next row. This will take the place of the ch 4 at beg of Row 2 of tunic front; turn.

Row 2: Ch 1, rep Row 2 of tunic front beg with first dc cluster in first ch-4 sp, end with dtr in 4th skipped ch; turn – 7 clusters total (2 dc clusters and 5 tr clusters).

Row 3: Rep Row 3 of front, end with last sc in next sc on back bodice, sl st in next 4 chs of next ch-4 sp on back bodice; turn – 13 ch-4 sps.

Row 4: Work same as Row 2, ending with dtr in top of dtr on row before last row; turn – 7 clusters.

Rows 5–35 (43, 51, 59): Rep rows 3 and 4, ending with a Row 3 rep. Make sure last sc on last row is worked in upper marked sc. Sl st in same sc. End off after last row.

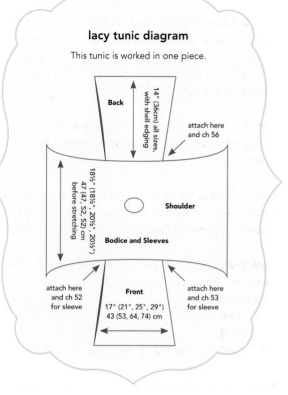

lacy tunic diagram

This tunic is worked in one piece.

Back

14" (36cm) all sizes, with shell edging

attach here and ch 56

18½" (18½", 20½", 20½") 47 (47, 52, 52) cm before stretching

Shoulder

Bodice and Sleeves

attach here and ch 52 for sleeve

Front
17" (21", 25", 29")
43 (53, 64, 74) cm

attach here and ch 53 for sleeve

seaming

With RS tog, sew sleeve and side seam, beg at end of sleeve and ending at 4th cluster on side (side slits formed). Rep on other sleeve and side.

optional edging: open shells

With RS facing, join yarn with sl st in st at bottom left-hand corner of tunic front, sc in same sp; * [ch 2, dc, ch 2, tr, ch 2, dc, ch 2] around post of next dtr (next to tr cluster), sc in top of next dtr; rep from * across front bottom edge, ending with last sc in st at bottom righthand corner. End off. Rep on bottom of tunic back. Number of open shells will be the same as number of cluster rows you worked. If desired, work shells on ends of sleeves in same manner.

finishing

Weave in ends. Add ribbon by weaving through spaces on bottom row of bodice. This tunic may need to be steam blocked.

CHAPTER FOUR

TWO~COLOR ACCESSORIES

Sometimes two colors are better than one. Re-create the timeless houndstooth check for a scarf or purse, or, for a look that's more vibrant, try a wave-stitch pattern that combines two contrasting but complementary colors.

SKILL LEVEL:

MEDIUM
4
MOYEN
Medio

1 BEGINNER

2 **ADVANCED BEGINNER**

3 INTERMEDIATE

The classic houndstooth-check pattern often comes in black and white, as seen in more dressy clothing and accessories. This purse shows a blue and taupe combination that could easily fit into an everyday casual look with jeans.

Felting this accessory gives it a wonderful finished look that highlights the pattern rather than individual stitches.

houndstooth-check felted purse

size

Before felting: approx 24" (61cm) wide (at widest point) x 10½" (27cm) tall (folded and lying flat)

After felting: approx 16" (41cm) wide (at widest point) x 6¾" (17cm) tall (folded and lying flat); 12½" (32cm) opening

materials

#4 medium worsted-weight yarn: 2 skeins blue and 1 skein taupe 100% wool or other natural fiber that will felt (3.5 oz/220 yd/100 g per skein)

Used in this project: Cascade 220 Peruvian highland wool yarn #9327 and #8408 (Substitute: Patons 100% Classic Merino Wool)

Size J/10 (6mm) crochet hook

1 set of purse handles

Snap for tabbed closure

1 decorative button for tab

⅓ yd (30cm) Peltex extra-firm stabilizer (optional)

½ yd (46cm) fabric for lining (optional)

Yarn needle

Sewing needle and thread to match lining fabric

4" x 12¼" (10cm x 31cm) box with plastic bag over it; laundry detergent; baking soda (for felting)

Tacky glue

gauge

Before felting, and crocheting loosely:

11 hdc = 4" (10cm)

10 hdc rows = 4" (10cm)

8 sts (alternating sc and dc) = 3" (8cm)

8 rnds (alternating blue and taupe) = 3" (8cm)

stitches used

ch, sl st, sc, hdc, dc

pattern notes

The houndstooth pattern is made by changing colors every rnd with graduated stitches of alternating sc and dc. All sts are worked in both lps.

Pattern stitch: Alternating sc, dc, sc, dc; next row – work dc in sc, and sc in dc.

instructions

purse bottom

Note: The bottom of the purse should measure approx 19" x 5" (48cm x 13cm) before felting.

With blue, ch 53.

Row 1: Hdc in 3rd ch from hook (skipped chs count as hdc), hdc in each rem ch across; turn – 52 hdc.

Row 2: Ch 2 (counts as hdc), sk first hdc, hdc in next hdc and in each hdc across, working last hdc in first skipped ch at beg of Row 1; turn – 52 hdc.

Rows 3–12: Ch 2 (counts as hdc), sk first hdc, hdc in next hdc and in each hdc across, working last hdc in 2nd ch of beg ch-2; turn – 52 hdc.

body of purse

Note: From the bottom of the purse, the body measures 10½" (27cm) tall × 24" (61cm) at its widest point when laying flat before felting. Leave blue lp on hook; drop blue yarn toward back of piece, but do not end off blue. Make a slipknot with taupe and place it on hook. Pull taupe through the blue lp. Leave blue yarn loose in back. It will be picked up at beg of Rnd 2.

Rnd 1: Working across short edge of bottom piece with taupe, ch 1; * sc around post of next hdc, dc around post of next hdc, rep from * across short edge – 12 sts on short edge.

Working along long edge, * sc in next st, dc in next st; rep from * across long edge – 52 sts on long edge.

Work 12 sts along next short edge and 52 sts along next long edge as before – 128 sts total.

Leave taupe lp on hook; drop taupe yarn toward back of piece, but do not end off. Pull blue through the taupe lp.

Rnd 2: With blue, (sl st, ch 2, dc) in first sc; * sc in next dc, dc in next sc; rep from * around, ending with sc in last dc – 128 sts. Let blue lie loose at back of work and pull taupe through blue lp.

Rnd 3: With taupe, (sl st, ch 1, sc) in first dc; * dc in next sc, sc in next dc; rep from * around, ending with dc in last sc. Drop taupe and pull blue through taupe lp.

Note: Blue rows will always begin with a dc and end with a sc. Taupe rows will always begin with a sc and end with a dc.

fibers for felting

When you want to felt any item, make sure you use 100% natural animal fibers, such as wool or yarn, that is meant for felting. Man-made fibers will not felt.

Rnds 4-28: Rep rnds 2 and 3, ending by working a Rnd 2 rep. End off after last rnd.

Note: For a taller purse, work more rnds. Two rnds = approx ½" (1cm) when felted, depending on the felting process.

before felting

purse tab

With blue, ch 9.

Row 1: Hdc in 3rd from hook (skipped chs count as hdc), hdc in each rem ch across; turn – 8 hdc.

Row 2: Ch 2 (counts as hdc), sk first hdc, hdc in next 6 hdc, hdc in first skipped ch on Row 1; turn – 8 hdc.

Row 3: Ch 2 (counts as hdc), sk first hdc, hdc in next 6 hdc, hdc in 2nd ch of beg ch-2; turn – 8 hdc.

Rows 4–14: Rep Row 3, 11 times more.

Row 15: Ch 2 (counts as hdc), sk first 2 hdc, hdc in next 3 hdc, sk next hdc, hdc in next hdc, leaving beg ch-2 unworked. End off. You'll have holes where the hdc were skipped, but they'll close up when felted – 5 hdc.

Tab will be sewn on after it is felted, so you can determine how long you want it to come in the front. Weave in loose ends.

felting

The purse in the photo on page 118 was felted so the stitches do not show, resembling fabric. Items can be felted in different ways, depending on how much you want the stitches to disappear or how much you want your item to shrink. Different washing machines and water temperatures may also cause an item to felt and shrink differently. You may only need to put your item through the wash once, or you may have to put it through a cycle up to 4 times. To felt this purse, follow these instructions.

Step 1: Place purse and tab inside zippered pillowcase. Put into washing machine on lowest water level and hottest setting. If water is not hot enough, turn up heat on water heater or pour boiling water into machine as it fills up. Place tennis shoes (or tennis balls) in washer to help with agitation. Add 1 tablespoon laundry detergent and ¼ cup baking soda. Run washing cycle. You may have to repeat this process 1–2 more times depending on the look you desire.

Step 2: Rinse in cold water; reshape and let spin to remove excess water.

Step 3: Before the felting process, have a 4" × 12¼" (10cm × 31cm) box ready with a plastic bag over it. (Have more than one size box ready in case the purse doesn't end up the size you expect.) Immediately place the wet purse onto the box, making sure it's a tight fit. Let it air dry completely for 2–3 days.

sewing on tab and handles

Tab: After purse is completely dry, sew beg edge of tab to inside of purse at center back with 1½" (4cm) of tab down inside purse. You can place tab down inside as far as you want, depending on how much you want your tab to show in the front and how tightly you want the tab to close the purse.

Handles: Place straight pins where you want handles to be sewn, approx 1½" (4cm) from top and 1½"–2" (4–5cm) from tab edges. Sew handles to front and back of purse with yarn and yarn needle.

adding optional lining

Cut stabilizer: for bottom – 1 piece 11½" × 3¼" (29cm × 8cm); for long sides – 2 pieces 11½" × 5¾" (29cm × 15cm) each

Note: If your purse did not end up the same size, cut your stabilizer pieces approx 1" (3cm) smaller than

the dimensions of the bottom and sides.

Glue each stabilizer piece to inside of purse with tacky glue, making sure you leave approx ½" (1cm) of purse edge showing at top. Cut a piece of lining fabric 18" × 19" (46cm × 48cm), or 1" (3cm) wider than purse and 1" (3cm) taller than top edges when lying flat). The extra 1" (3cm) of fabric at the top of each side will be folded over to be sewn inside purse. Fold fabric in half so it will measure 18" × 9½" (46 × 24cm). Sew ½" (1cm) wide seams on short sides, leaving long, top edge open. Fold will be at bottom inside purse. Place lining inside purse and adjust to fit if necessary. Fold top edge of lining over approx 1"–1½" (3cm–4cm) toward WS of purse to fit, leaving about ¼" (1cm) of purse showing on inside. Pin lining to purse around inside top edge and hand sew in place with needle and thread.

after felting

finishing

Tuck center top of purse ends to inside and tack fold together to secure. Sew button to top front of tab. Mark placement of snap, and sew one side of snap to front of purse and other side of snap to back of tab.

try a houndstooth-check scarf

Flip to the next page to make a nonfelted, houndstooth-check scarf that's perfect for men or women. The color combination used is just one of many possible. Made with single-crochet and double-crochet stitches, this advanced-beginner scarf is not difficult at all to create, but pay a little more attention as you work: You will be alternating stitches and it would be easy to miss a stitch.

houndstooth-check scarf

size

5" x 52" (13cm x 132cm) or desired length

materials

#4 medium worsted-weight yarn: 1 skein
(3.5 oz/223 yd/100 g) gray; 1 skein (3.5 oz/
170 yd/100 g) green

Used in this project: Patons 100% Classic Merino
Wool in Dark Grey; Lion Brand Vanna's Choice
acrylic in Dusty Green

Size J/10 (6mm) crochet hook

Yarn needle

gauge

6 sts (alternating sc and dc) and 6 rows =
2" (5cm)

6 rows = 2⅜" (6cm)

stitches used

ch, sc, dc

pattern notes

All sts are worked in both lps. See page 17 for
instructions on how to change yarn color on the
last stitch of each row.

instructions

With gray, ch 16.

Row 1: With gray, sc in 2nd ch from hook, * dc in
next ch, sc in next ch; rep from * across. Change
to green on last 2 lps of last sc. End off gray,
leaving a 6" (15cm) tail; turn – 15 sts.

Row 2: With green, ch 3 (counts as first dc); sk
first sc, * sc in next dc, dc in next sc; rep from
* across. Change to gray on last 2 lps of last dc.
End off green, leaving a 6" (15cm) tail;
turn – 15 sts.

Row 3: With gray, ch 1; sc in first dc; * dc in next sc,
sc in next dc; rep from * across, ending with sc in 3rd
ch of beg ch-3. Change to green on last 2 lps of last sc.
End off gray, leaving a 6" (15cm) tail; turn – 15 sts.

Rep rows 2 and 3, 65 times more, for desired length.
At end of last row, do not change colors. End off.
Weave in loose ends.

SKILL LEVEL:

MEDIUM
4
MOYEN
Medio

1 BEGINNER

2 **ADVANCED
BEGINNER**

3 INTERMEDIATE

The graduated stitches in this pattern result in a particularly beautiful piece when you use two complementary colors. You can use the same pattern to make a larger purse or even a scarf. The wave stitch isn't difficult, but closely follow the stitch diagram on page 125 to avoid making mistakes.

wave-stitch coin purse

size

6½" x 4" (17cm x 10cm)

materials

#4 medium worsted-weight yarn: 1 skein (3 oz/ 165 yd) green; 1 skein (5 oz/256 yd/140 g) purple

Used in this project: Caron Simply Soft acrylic in Dark Sage; Red Heart Soft Yarn (acrylic) in Grape

Size F/5 (3.75mm) crochet hook

¼ yd (23cm) fabric for lining (optional)

1 green zipper, 7" (18cm) long (optional)

1–3 large beads for pulling zipper closed (optional)

Peltex extra-firm fusible stabilizer (optional)

Yarn needle

Sewing needle and thread to match lining and zipper (optional)

gauge

5 sc = 1" (3cm)

2 sc rows = ⅜" (1cm)

1 oval-shaped pattern consisting of 2 purple rows = 2" x 1" (5cm x 3cm)

stitches used

ch, sc, hdc, dc, tr

pattern notes

Sts are worked in both lps. Try working your stitches tight so the coin purse will be firmer. You have the option of adding a lining and a zipper.

For a scarf: Work the stitches much looser so it will be soft. Repeat rows 2–9 as many times as needed to make a scarf with horizontal rows (same as the coin purse). Or form long vertical rows by working your beginning chain as long as desired in multiples of 12 plus 11.

instructions

purse sides (make 2)

With green, ch 35.

Row 1: (RS) Sc in 2nd ch from hook and in each ch rem across; turn – 34 sc.

Row 2: Ch 1, sc in each sc across, changing to purple on last 2 lps of last st (see page 17 for how to change yarn colors). Do not end off green. Let it lie loose to be picked up at the end of Row 4; turn – 34 sc.

Row 3: With purple, ch 3 (counts as dc), sk first sc, dc in next sc, hdc in next sc, sc in next sc; * ch 2, sk next 2 sc, sc in next sc, hdc in next sc, dc in next 2 sc, tr in next 2 sc, dc in next 2 sc, hdc in next sc, sc in next sc; rep from

* to across last 6 sc; ch 2, sk next 2 sc, sc in next sc, hdc in next sc, dc in last 2 sc, turn – 28 sts and 3 ch-2 sps.

Row 4: Ch 3, sk first dc, dc in next dc, hdc in next hdc, sc in next sc; * ch 2, sk next ch-2 sp, sc in next sc, hdc in next hdc, dc in next 2 dc, tr in next 2 tr, dc in next 2 dc, hdc in next hdc, sc in next sc; rep from * across to last 6 sts; ch 2, sk next ch-2 sp, sc in next sc, hdc in next hdc, dc in next dc, dc in 3rd ch of beg ch-3, changing to green on last 2 lps of last st as before, allowing purple to lie loose; turn – 28 sts and 3 ch-2 sps.

Row 5: With green, ch 1, sc in first 4 sts; working around ch-2 sps on previous 2 rows, sc in 2 skipped sc 3 rows below (green row); * sc in next 10 sts on previous row, sc in 2 skipped sc 3 rows below; rep

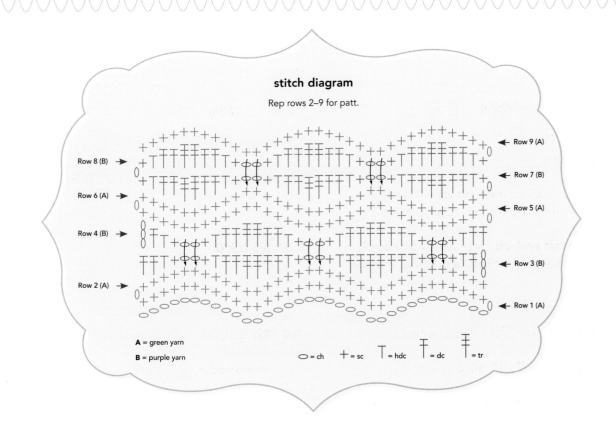

stitch diagram

Rep rows 2–9 for patt.

Row 8 (B) →
← Row 9 (A)
← Row 7 (B)
Row 6 (A) →
← Row 5 (A)
Row 4 (B) →
← Row 3 (B)
Row 2 (A) →
← Row 1 (A)

A = green yarn
B = purple yarn

○ = ch   + = sc   T = hdc   ⊤ = dc   ⊥ = tr

from * across to last 4 sts; sc in next 3 sts, sc in 3rd ch of beg ch-3; turn – 34 sc.

Row 6: Ch 1, sc in each sc across, changing to purple on last st; turn – 34 sc.

Row 7: With purple, ch 1, sc in first sc; * hdc in next sc, dc in next 2 sc, tr in next 2 sc, dc in next 2 sc, hdc in next sc, sc in next sc, ch 2, sk next 2 sc; sc in next sc; rep from * across, omitting ch-2 and sc at end of last rep; turn – 30 sts.

Row 8: Ch 1, sc in first sc, * hdc in next hdc, dc in next 2 dc, tr in next 2 tr, dc in next 2 dc, hdc in next hdc, sc in next sc, ch 2; sk next ch-2 sp, sc in next sc; rep from * across, omitting ch-2 and sc at end of last rep and changing to green on last st; turn – 30 sts and 2 ch-2 sps.

Row 9: With green, ch 1, sc in first 10 sts; * working around ch-2 sps on previous 2 rows, sc in 2 skipped sc 3 rows below; sc in next 10 sts; rep from * across; turn – 34 sc.

Rows 10–17: Rep rows 2–9.

Row 18: Rep Row 2. Do not change color at end of row. End off.

optional stabilizer

Cut 2 pieces of fusible stabilizer approx ½" (1cm) smaller than purse sides. Fuse to WS of purse sides as per manufacturer instructions.

With RS tog, match up sts and sew seams at sides and bottom of purse, leaving long edge open at top. Turn RS out.

optional lining and zipper

Lining: Cut 2 pieces of lining fabric ½" (1cm) wider than purse width and height on 3 sides, but 1" (3cm) taller at top, so it can be folded over for hand-sewing into purse. Sew ¼" (1cm) seams on sides and bottom, leaving top edge open. Place lining down inside purse and fold top edge over toward inside of purse. Take out lining and press folded edge at top. Place back down inside purse and hand-stitch to inside top edge with sewing needle and thread.

Zipper: Pin zipper to top edges of lining and hand-stitch in place. Place 1–3 beads on yarn and tie a knot at one end to keep beads in place. Attach other end of yarn to hole in zipper pull and secure.

RESOURCES

I want to thank all the yarn companies who were so generous in supplying yarn for the designs in this book.

Bernat, Patons and Lily Yarns
320 Livingstone Ave. S.
Listowel, Ontario,
Canada N4W 3H3
(888) 368-8401
bernat.com
patonsyarns.com
lilyyarns.com

Caron International
P.O. Box 222
Washington, NC 27889
caron.com

Cascade Yarns
(206) 574-0440
cascadeyarns.com

Coats & Clark
(J&P Coats)
P.O. Box 12229
Greenville, SC 29612
(800) 648-1479
coatsandclark.com

Crochet Style Etc.
(Hilos Omega nylon
crochet cord and
Sinfonia cotton yarn)
6278 Youngland Dr.
Columbus, OH 43228
(614) 205-3210
crochetstyleetc.com

Crystal Palace Yarns
160 S. 23rd St.
Richmond, CA 94804
(510) 237-9988
straw.com
crystalpalaceyarns.com

Hobby Lobby Creative Centers (Yarn Bee Yarns)
7717 SW 44th St.
Oklahoma City, OK 73179
(405) 745-1200
hobbylobby.com
craftsetc.com

Interlacements Yarns
P.O. Box 3082
Colorado Springs,
CO 80934
(719) 578-8009
interlacementsyarns.com

Lion Brand Yarn
135 Kero Rd.
Carlstadt, NJ 07072
(800) 258-9276
lionbrand.com

Plymouth Yarn Company, Inc.
500 Lafayette St.
Bristol, PA 19007
(215) 788-0459
plymouthyarn.com

South West Trading Company
(866) 794-1818
soysilk.com

WEBS – America's Yarn Store
Kathy Elkins
75 Service Center Rd.
Northampton, MA 01060
(800) 367-9327
yarn.com

Westminster Fibers, Inc.
Yarn Division
165 Ledge St.
Nashua, NH 03060
(800) 445-9276
westminsterfibers.com

YarnSmiths
1230 Mitchell Blvd.
Springfield, OH 45503
(888) 550-5648
yarnsmiths.com

Busy Beaver Arts & Crafts
3445 Dayton-Xenia Rd.
Dayton, OH 45432
(937) 429-3920

Arlene Graham's Fiberworks
4013 Dayton-Xenia Rd.
Beavercreek, OH 45432
(937) 429-9276
fiberworksdayton.com

Hancock Fabrics
1 Fashion Way
Baldwyn, MS 38824
(877) 322-7427
hancockfabrics.com

JoAnn Fabric and Craft Stores
5555 Darrow Rd.
Hudson, OH 44236
(888) 739-4120
joann.com

Michaels Stores, Inc.
8000 Bent Branch Dr.
Irving, TX 75063
(800) 642-4235
michaels.com

Prism Arts, Inc.
prismyarn.com

Tilli Tomas
Boston, MA 02130
(617) 524-3330
tillitomas.com

INDEX

DISCOVER A WORLD OF STITCHING IDEAS

Positively Crochet!
50 Fashionable Projects
and Inspirational Tips
by Mary Jane Hall
Create 50 fashion-forward projects, including scarves, shrugs, sweaters, hats, jewelry and more, using the tips and stitches showcased in this inspirational guide.

Paperback, 8-1/4" x 10-7/8", 128 pages
ISBN-13: 978-0-89689-517-1
ISBN-10: 0-89689-517-3
#Z0821

Carry Alongs
15 Crochet Handbags & Purses
for Every Occasion
by Carrie A. Sullivan
Delivers simple instructions and encouragement for creating 15 crocheted handbags, including evening bags, beach bags, drawstring designs, elegant shoulder bags and more, all made with today's fashion-forward yarns.

Paperback, 8-1/2" x 11", 96 pages
ISBN-13: 978-0-89689-656-7
ISBN-10: 0-89689-656-0
#Z2064

Felted Crochet
by Jane Davis
This resource provides step-by-step instructions for easily creating 30 beautiful accents for home and wardrobe, including purses, bags, blankets, pillows, a vest and more.

Paperback, 8-1/4" x 10-7/8", 128 pages
ISBN-13: 978-0-87349-887-6
ISBN-10: 0-87349-887-9
#FELCR

Join a world of crafters at
www.mycraftivity.com.

Connect. Create. Explore.

Easy Crocheted Accessories
by Carol Meldrum
Create 20 chic crocheted items including bags, ponchos, scarves, throws and gloves with the guidance of detailed instructions and 200 brilliant color photos.

Paperback, 7-1/2" x 9-3/4", 128 pages
ISBN-13: 978-0-89689-275-0
ISBN-10: 0-89689-275-1
#ECA

Easy to Crochet Cute
Clothes For Kids
by Sue Whiting
Explore the versatility of crochet as you create 25 easy outfits and accessories for babies and toddlers, using a variety of contemporary yarns.

Paperback, 10" x 8-1/4", 128 pages
ISBN-13: 978-0-89689-588-1
ISBN-10: 0-89689-588-2
#Z1439